Live Inspired

Laura Staley

Copyright © 2020

All rights reserved.

This book or part thereof may not be reproduced in any form, stored in a retrieval system, or transmitted in any form by any means-electronic, mechanical, photocopy, recording, or otherwise without prior written permission of the publisher, except as provided by United States of America copyright law.

The information provided in this book is designed to provide helpful information on the subjects discussed. This book is not meant to be used, nor should it be used, to diagnose or treat any medical condition. The author and publisher are not responsible for any specific health needs that may require medical supervision and are not liable for any damages or negative consequences from any treatment, action, application, or preparation, to any person reading or following the information in this book.

References are provided for information purposes only and do not constitute endorsement of any websites or other sources. In the event you use any of the information in this book for yourself, the author and the publisher assume no responsibility for your actions.

Books may be purchased through booksellers or by contacting Sacred Stories Publishing.

Live Inspired
Laura Staley
Tradepaper ISBN: 978-1-945026-64-5
Electronic ISBN: 978-1-945026-65-2

Library of Congress Control Number: 2020933225

Published by Sacred Stories Publishing, Fort Lauderdale, FL
Printed in the United States of America

For Julianna and Matthew
I Love You Both Forever and Always

TABLE OF CONTENTS

SECTION ONE: Living Awake

Open Spaces iii
The Soul of Silence 1
A Pathway to a Quieter Mind 9
Listen to Your Body 15
Liberate Yourself 21
The Importance of Unravelling 25
The Death of Pretending 33
Dishwasher Running 37
It Is Not Personal 41
In My Mind, My Dog Was Dying 45
Lost My Voice, Found Myself, Again 49
Exoskeleton 55

SECTION TWO: Living True

The Voice of Courage 59
Courage at the Core 63
Pay Attention to the Truth 69
Perceptions of Others 75
Breaking Free 79
The Dance of Trust and Discernment 85
The Practice of Patience 91
The Courage to Be You 97

Being Seen, Heard, and Valued 103
Love Heals 109
Belong to Yourself.. 113
Boundaries 119

SECTION THREE: Living Joyously
Love Aligns... 125
Finding Joy in the Messes of Life...................................... 127
Snafus and Serendipity 131
Ladder Clatter 137
Gratitude as a Catalyst 143
Flight Wings of Kindness 149
Allow Joy to Lift You 153
He Had Me at Mary Oliver 157
Hang On—Help Is On Its Way 163
Create Space for Joy 167
Live Like It Matters... 173
Magical Mountain 179

SECTION FOUR: Living Beyond
Soar.. 185
A Fresh Start... 187
A Beautiful Interior by Design 193

Surfing the Net of Opportunity 197
Standing for Love 201
Becoming Whole 205
The World as You Are 211
From Traumas to Quiet Triumph 217
Breakthroughs in Being Alive 221
Live an Ordinary, Exceptional Life 227
Get Your House in Order 231
Weaving Themes Together 237
Breathe and Be 241

AFTERWORD 243
ACKNOWLEDGMENTS: A Grateful Heart 249
ABOUT THE AUTHOR 255

SECTION ONE

Living Awake

Open Spaces

Remove the shards
Of shattered glass
From your arteries,
The heavy blanket of
Hot sweaty
Shame from your
Rounded shoulders,
The shackles of
Past betrayals
From
Your ankles.

Find your heart in
The empty, the full
Deep in desire.

Flow free this love
Like cascading waterfalls
Into all the broken open
Spaces of your soul.

The creases, bumps
Lumps of your head.
The lines, wrinkles,
Crepe paper of your skin.

Fill all the tributaries
Of veins with
Kindness,
Tenderness.

Pour into
Soft eyes
Aching, yearning,
Searching for this
Thirst to be quenched.

Rush like a tidal
Wave, a storm
Surge your
Passion to all.

Soak into your bones
Saturated, drenched
This flood that
Spills
Over.

Who do you want
To be in the open spaces?

Who will be there
When you arrive?

A
Vast
Luscious
Ocean of
Liberation.

The Soul of Silence

"Words can make a deeper scar than silence can heal."
—*Unknown*

As a child, I felt a cautious relief from walking on eggshells when my mother played the grand piano in our living room. Playing the piano seemed to make her happy while shifting her focus away from me. She especially enjoyed playing "Begin the Beguine."

My older sister, who played the piano with similar ease and skill, took lessons with a music professor who was an accomplished pianist. My sister often practiced in the evening when I was in bed. The sweet music of my sister playing "Claire De Lune" wafted through the air, helping to soothe my anxious body.

One day when I was six years old, I danced around in my white tights and red corduroy jumper as my older sister played the piano. I yearned to make my fingers tap those black and white keys. I asked my mother if I could take lessons. She said, "Well, you'll never play the piano like your sister does!" I didn't mind; I still wanted to learn. I asked again daily for a week. Finally, she told me she had scheduled piano lessons for me. I was anxious but also thrilled.

On the day of my first lesson, my mother drove me to the home of my piano teacher, introduced me, and left. The old woman, who was polite and kind to my mother, morphed into this terrifying witch toward me. "Sit down!" Her brittle words crackled around me as terror consumed my body. I complied with her order. Sitting on the piano bench, I barely took a breath.

She grabbed my left hand, turned it over. Smack! A ruler stung my palm.

"Curved fingers over those keys!" She grabbed my right hand. Thwack. Bowing their heads, my trembling fingertips timidly pressed on the keys.

White and black blurred as hot tears bubbled out of my eyes. My body imprisoned my terrified, wailing self as the saltwater streamed down my cheeks. The piano teacher bellowed, "Stop crying and play these notes!" This continued until my mother returned.

I pulled on my coat when my mother arrived. My red, swollen hands clutched the piano book I was told to take home with me to practice. My fear moved to my belly.

The Soul of Silence

In the backseat of the car, the cold vinyl seeped through my tights into my thighs and bottom. My mother's words swirled around me.

"Your piano teacher is such a wonderful lady! You should be so grateful getting to learn piano from her. You know you'll need to practice every day…"

I squeezed my eyes shut to dam the leaks. I knew I had to remain silent about my experience with the mean piano teacher. My mother wouldn't have believed me. She would have accused me of being ungrateful, and her reality ruled.

Somehow my burning desire to learn to play this instrument percolated to the surface the next afternoon. I sat at the piano to practice. My mother appeared out of nowhere at my left shoulder.

"Sit up straight! Curve your fingers! Don't push so hard on the keys! You're banging on the keys! That is not playing! That sounds awful! You will never play like your sister! Didn't I tell you that? Now practice!"

Tears streamed down my face. I didn't feel my fingers on the keys, but I heard strings pinging as she continued to holler. After what felt like eternity, she walked to the kitchen.

From the moment I returned from school each day until she heard me playing the piano, my mother stalked my resistance. No matter where she was, her scolding, nagging words filled the house until the tiny gauze-wrapped hammers struck the strings of steel deep in the belly of the piano. My body dragged itself into the living room for days of this ritual.

After several weeks of this torture from my mother and piano teacher, I walked into the foyer of our home after school and was met by my mother.

"It's time to practice piano, Laurie!"

Feeling like I was moving through mud, I made my way to the piano bench and sat dead still. Her chiding turned to rage as she stormed into the room.

"We are paying all this money for you to learn how to play. Shame on you for not practicing enough, you ungrateful, selfish, shithead of a child!"

Weeks of hurt and fear erupted out of me as anger. I jumped up from the bench glaring directly at her hate-filled face.

"I don't want to take piano lessons. I won't go anymore, ever!"

She yelled louder. "You are a failure, a worthless piece of shit, a disgrace to our family!"

I ran from the room, not feeling my legs.

That night, I buried myself under the covers of my bed, ready for sleep. My dad came to my bedside, pulled the covers back from my head. I knew what he wanted; we had done this drill many times.

"You need to apologize to your mother, Laurie. You made her cry. We're really disappointed in you."

My anger whispered in my head: *When did she cry? I never saw her cry. If she did it would come out as either steam or icicles!*

Then guilt and remorse flooded my body along with hurt and confusion; my brain disconnected. I trudged down the carpeted stairway and stood outside the open door of my parents' bedroom. My feet felt bound to the wood floor.

"I'm sorry, Mommy." I stared into the black opening like wounded prey at the mouth of a vicious bear's cave. Stillness. I didn't even hear her breathing.

After this, the piano lessons with the mean old lady ended. The icy silence from my mom deepened as she withdrew from me. I became invisible to her, completely shunned until her next unpredictable tongue lashing. The piano in the living room glared at me as guilt, shame, and terror entombed my shattered desire.

Understandably, knowing when to remain silent, when to speak up, when to let another's words not slice into my heart became a painful learning curve throughout most of my life and eventually a healthy practice over time. Learning to trust, discern, and lean into my own experiences rather than what adults told me I was supposed to think and feel about reality took years. I often doubted my own truths because they were constantly denied, rewritten, or questioned. I grew up with "Navy Seal-like" training from shape-shifting adults, unpredictable in their interactions with me. It's a lie that only sticks and stones can hurt you. Rage-filled words can do great harm to children, especially those who are tender-hearted and introverted.

Some of you may have learned to be silent, but on the inside your mind and heart fill to overflowing with words and feelings. You know all too well the experience of stuffing your words, "biting your tongue," or burying your honest emotions. Did you create a safe place to purge thoughts and feelings, or do they still chatter or burn inside of you right now as you read these words?

In contrast, you may observe that you talk incessantly with no filter, no internal editor sitting with her red pen at the desk of your voice box. Any thought that bubbles up inside of you comes bouncing right off your tongue. There's no dress rehearsal or pause button. You notice you're reactive. You're quick to speak your mind, to express your feelings.

Cultivating an ability to listen deeply becomes an exquisite gift of unconditional love you give to another human being. Listening from stillness with an open mind and an open heart allows infinite space for another human being to weep, to breathe, to hear themselves, to uncover their own truth, to be broken and whole, lost, and to be exactly who they are in that moment. To listen with presence can make another individual feel like they are the most beloved being in the entire Universe. Wrapping them in a warm, soft blanket of your undivided attention, you become a sacred gift given from the soul of silence.

May you become this rare and wonderous treasure for yourself, for others, and for our world.

A Pathway to a Quieter Mind

"Let silence be the art you practice."
—Rumi

Why have I been so exhausted? Why didn't I get invited to that social event? Why did I ask that clerk such a stupid question? She looked at me with such disdain after I spoke to her! Why can't I ever remember to say or do the right thing? I am such a dumbass, a sh*thead. I can be such an idiot! Did I pay the electric bill? I really am a worthless piece of s*&^!

In graduate school, my internal chatterbox became powerful and mean. One evening my parents and my boyfriend's mother came over for dinner. As we sat eating our meal of broiled chicken, green beans, and wild rice, the topic of our living together got spoken about with fierce judgment from my mother.

"When are the two of you getting married and putting an end to this disgraceful situation?"

From the day we moved to our apartment, my mother began mailing me pamphlets and books about the sins of living together, the evils of having sex outside of the sanctity of marriage. Sections of the books were underlined with exclamation points in the margins with demeaning words about me.

The man I was "shacking up" with and I looked at each other. We put down our forks. He began a thoughtful, reasonable explanation of our choice, one he and I had discussed many times. I chimed in with my thoughts, which included that I was a grown adult and capable of making decisions for myself. I also added that she had a right to her point of view, that I had known her perspective for a long time. My dad wanted to know my boyfriend's intentions. His mom spoke up before he could answer my dad.

"I think they have every right to choose what they choose. I love your daughter, and I love my son. They are both adults, and their living situation is none of my business. My son is a good man with a good heart. Please refrain from questioning his intentions."

Then all hell broke loose as my mother unleashed her poisonous righteousness, mostly directed at me. His mom stood up, put her napkin on the table, and announced she needed to leave. My boyfriend and I both stood up. My boyfriend's mom walked over and hugged her son. Then she looked at me.

"Thank you so much for cooking this delicious meal, for inviting me to your home. I'm so sorry to have to leave abruptly, but I will not sit and listen to this."

I walked to get her coat, relieved to have a task, to remove myself from my mother's toxic energy field. As I walked into the foyer, my mother yelled, again, "I did not raise you to be a whore!"

Burning with shame, a familiar nausea in my belly, I handed his mother her coat. I barely looked at her as I mumbled, "Thank you for coming over." She hugged me briefly and left.

Somehow my dad managed to shift the conversation to politics with my boyfriend as they made their way to the foyer to get my dad's and mom's coats. From the hallway, I observed my mom walking into our kitchen with the dishes. She obviously saw the bumper sticker on our fridge "Arms Are for Hugging," because she spoke these words in her fake syrupy voice. Then she turned and walked to the foyer with arms opened wide towards me. I reluctantly acquiesced, feeling her fake hug, while hearing more cruel words spoken into my ear. I wept bitterly after they left.

A few days later when I felt terrified about having thoughts of putting a gun to my head, I knew I had to deal with my internal bully. Breaking the fierce rule of "what happens in our family stays in our family," I bravely walked into the Ohio State Health Clinic and booked an appointment with one of the mental health counselors. This began a long journey of disconnecting from the bully that lived in my mind, eventually healing the trauma that resided in my body, and ultimately choosing to be unresponsive to my entire family of origin.

Maybe you also have an internal bully who makes you feel like you aren't good enough, or maybe in your case it's a chatterbox who nags you about every little thing. The bothersome inner voice may be an anxious worrier who reminds you of every bad thing that could happen in even the happiest situation, or this voice may be self-pitying or martyr-like. For some of you, the voice inside is an overthinker who must explore everything from multiple angles, even if you're trying to sleep or complete a task. For many people, the inner voice is a mix of many of these. Maybe you wish, as I did, that there was a way to take a vacation from the activity in your mind that makes it difficult to focus on things you need to do or who you want to be.

What if you could just notice your inner voice? What if you could cultivate a "fly on the wall" – the part of you that notices your thoughts, body sensations, and feelings? This part of you can grow and expand a capacity to quietly watch you do you. Shifting to this silent witness allows you to pay attention from a broader perspective, from the seat of your awakened self. Over time, a transformation can take place in what you see including things, thoughts, people, and places.

May you find a quieter mind that creates breathing room for this moment that you are alive. May you find your way to your heart to listen to the wisdom that lives there.

Listen to Your Body

"The body says what words cannot."
—Martha Graham,
The Mother of Modern Dance

Walking up the flights of steps during my senior year in college to the 4th floor dance studio in Edgar Hall, I anticipated the expanse of time and silence to move in my leotard- and tights-clad body to the inner rhythms of my being. Sunlight often streamed through the bank of windows on the south facing wall. The mirrors on the east wall reflected this light which cast my body in a moving, flowing shadow on the floor. I watched in wonder as a witness to my own movement and shapes. I experienced delightful shadow dancing in the warmth and quiet of this space. I stopped, sat down, opened my notebook, grabbed a pencil, and sketched diagrams of these body movements as a dance unfolded through my beating heart, breath, and imagination. A theme of hand movement emerged. Hands had fascinated me for a long time.

These moments of quiet permission to create a beginning, middle, and end of an artistic expression reunited me with my middle school self, who danced in this same studio with Dale Scholl's modern dance classes. With Ms. Scholl's gentle, yet passionate guidance, one of my best friends and I found a place, a respite of empowered connection to our awkward, girl-changing-into-young-lady bodies.

This second opportunity to choreograph arrived after three years of being selected to be a member of the Orchesis Dance Company, directed by Dance Professor Mary Titus. Ms. Titus, a fireball of energy, believed passionately in the artist inside of us dancers. She demonstrated this gift of silently noting a lack of self-worth that showed in our body postures and choosing purposefully to speak to the heart of movement, the power of potential in releasing what might be holding us back. She remains an adult woman in my life who saw my goodness, beauty, and raw potential through eyes of compassion, a heart committed to the birth of my confidence. The desire to spark her enthusiastic cheers matched the unbridled liberation I experienced in creating and teaching my dancers this new dance.

Honored to have my dance piece be the final one of our annual performance, I stood off-stage by the curtain as my dancers took the floor of the main stage of the Chappelear Drama Center. The lights came up, shining on the dancers' amazing sculpted bodies. Their colorful, simple leotards of beautiful shades of red-like fingernail polish caught the eye without distracting from the shapes as they moved together and apart. I took deep breaths as they deliciously executed what had just months ago existed secretly inside of me. Towards the end, a little boy burst out laughing at their movement, which seemed to give the entire audience permission to belly-laugh. The movement was utterly comical, which inspired the title "Out of Hand." Oh, to be off-stage knowing that something I created through these beautiful, skilled dancers' bodies brought joy to an entire room full of people felt like an utterly humbling joy, an awakened light of gratitude. A few years later I wept when I learned that Mary Titus died.

For years in my adulthood, I walked around like a disconnected talking head, sometimes a bobblehead, seemingly devoid of a torso, legs, or feet. I'm not quite certain what anchored me to the ground. If someone had asked me to feel my feet without touching my toes with my hands, I would've looked at them with my "WTF?!?!" face.

Living seemingly only in my mind, I attempted to solve ridiculous riddles that had nothing to do with anything, visited many past conversations with "I wish I had …," muttered mean things about myself, worried, or simmered.

All this busyness in my headspace kept me distracted from feeling the clothes on my body or my abdomen expanding when I inhaled. Did I even know if my feet got cold? In my rigorous efforts to cope, I had forgotten the tiny dancer, the choreographer inside of me.

What is your body saying to you? What are your feet, knees, or neck whispering? What are your eyelashes communicating? If they could speak, what would they say? What's gurgling in your intestines right now besides your breakfast or lunch? What's in your throat? Does the cat have your tongue right next to the catnip? If your heart held a megaphone, what would it declare?

An important and empowering relationship exists between the body-mind, which includes the heart, and consciousness, that part of you quietly noticing the screen of your laptop or holding this book in your hands. The nervous, muscular, skeletal, digestive, respiratory, and endocrine systems miraculously salsa dance together inside of you every day. Experiencing life through your body can expand your capacity to heal, to enjoy life, to be here in this sacred moment, to discover new information about being human. Your body wisdom can guide you towards deeper realizations, truths about who you are, who you are becoming, and transformations.

Can you right now drop into your body? Are you able to relax all parts of yourself from your clenched jaw to your curled toes? During your next meal, can you taste and savor the food you place in your mouth – the textures, the temperature, the spice, sweet, or savory? What if you stood up, stretched your arms up in a V for victory? What might you observe? Do you notice the cool air entering your nostrils? Can you trust your body, your inner emotional GPS to inspire your next actions, even if you have no idea what might happen tomorrow?

May you find that lifeforce inside your body where you can sit quietly to listen. May your body wisdom lead the way to wholeness, fulfillment, joy of the integrated kind, and to where words cannot venture.

Liberate Yourself

"Every aspect of your life is energetically anchored in your living space, so clearing clutter can transform your entire existence."
—Karen Kingston

It was New Year's Day. Now married to my second husband and a mother to two young children, I drove our family vehicle loaded to the hilt with all kinds of objects that my parents had given me over the years. A teakettle, a robe, small pieces of furniture, some appliances, artwork, books, videos, tapes, magazines, skirts, dresses, jewelry, and sweaters all rode with me. My parents' house was thirty minutes away. I pulled up their driveway, got out, walked onto their porch, and rang the doorbell. I returned to the van and began unloading. My parents opened the door and walked onto their porch. My mother spoke with a certain joy.

"You've left your second husband! You are moving home!"

My dad looked confused, lost.

I silently grabbed items and walked them up the steps and through their front door. I placed them in the foyer. My dad finally realized that he could join me in the process of unloading my Honda Odyssey minivan. We worked as a team. I tuned out my mother's prattle. The last action I took was to hand them a thank-you letter I had written before I left my home. I hugged them. "Happy New Year! I love you." I scampered off the porch and reversed my van down their narrow driveway.

Earlier that day, I sat in my recliner that I called my peace chair, reading a passage in *Conversations with God* by Neale Donald Walsh. A huge "AHA" rose up inside of me…his discussion of unconditional love, that it is an experience distinct from conditional love, that it is an energy experience…in this moment I knew the energy field of every single object my mom gave me was toxic. Gifts were weapons in my mother's arsenal, and she used them regularly. The promise of a love gift became a twisted game of bait and switch. She'd ask what I wanted. Next, she'd tell me I did not want whatever I had said. Then she'd deliver a "gift" that consistently created a profound confusion inside of me. "How dare you think you'd get what *you* want!" landed loud and clear.

The demand to be thanked showed itself as a terrifying storm including the inevitable tongue-lashing of my character. No matter how often or thoroughly I flooded appreciation her way, she consistently assaulted me with the words, "You are an ungrateful, selfish bitch!" When my mother visited our home, she regularly roared ever-changing use and care instructions for these belongings that I unknowingly completely failed to follow. The realization rose up inside me: I can give them all back to her! Every one of the "gifts" contained painful associations. These belongings had never been given freely and unconditionally from the heart.

With these items gone, the house we lived in could begin to feel like our home rather than an outpost for belongings that triggered my mother's cruel outbursts. Over the next few hours, it slowly dawned on me that I never, ever had to accept a "gift" from her again. Not ever.

On this new day of a new year, I drove away as they opened the envelope with the letter that said, "Thank you so much for all of these items. It was so generous of you to allow me to have them. I am so grateful to have had them in my life, but I no longer need any of them. I realize they were never given unconditionally, so you can now have them back. Thank you, again! Happy New Year! Love, Laura."

Clutter can show up in your physical space as unused belongings. The items might be associated with emotional stories that you struggle to resolve. You may think that you are your past and all the objects associated with your past. These belongings may have wonderful associations or heartbreaking meanings, but these items are not you. They tell stories about your life, but they aren't *you*.

Sometimes staying attached to things seems easier than remaining connected with people in your life. Like a child clinging to a stuffed animal, sometimes you make a deeper emotional investment in inanimate objects than in people. These objects usually don't talk, yell, rage, cry, bully, or cruelly shame you. Holding a book can seem more comfortable than holding someone's hand. You might avert your eyes from people and look for a long time at your cell phone.

Your emotions can show you what you actually care about. You wouldn't have all these feelings if you weren't committed to something or someone. The intensity of your grief, loneliness, or shame associated with clutter often points to the depth of your commitment, your love, and your desire to belong in a meaningful, healthy way.

I wish you deep and enduring peace as you take those gentle actions to clear your life of clutter as best as you can in this moment. May you liberate yourself!

The Importance of Unravelling

"...feelings like disappointment, embarrassment, irritation, resentment, anger, jealousy, and fear, instead of being bad news, are actually very clear moments that teach us where it is that we're holding back. They teach us to perk up and lean in when we feel we'd rather collapse and back away. They're like messengers that show us, with terrifying clarity, exactly where we're stuck. This very moment is the perfect teacher, and lucky for us, it's with us wherever we are."
—Pema Chödrön

While engaged in transformational work, I distinguished a part of myself that felt like a psycho bitch from hell, my rage. I named her Lois. Most of the time I could be patient and loving with my young children until I just wasn't. The constant buzz of hypervigilance and high anxiety raced in the background of my being until it didn't. Home from grocery shopping, I carried our son in the Baby Bjorn and walked with our three-year-old daughter into the kitchen. She chatted with me about pre-school, clapped her hands, covered her eyes, uncovered them and said, "Obbghfutf," making our son laugh.

"Baby! Baby!" she chanted.

I lifted him out of the carrier to crawl and sit as he pleased on the floor. My legs became a Maypole as the kids weaved in, out, under and around my legs and feet as I put away more groceries. Yet despite this playful interaction, I felt the inner rumblings, the brewing of that psycho bitch rage. Lois roared to the surface.

Like a bolt of lightning of alien invasion, Lois, now on full volume, electrified my whole body. I barely noticed my then husband, standing in the doorway, bearing witness to this cartoonish, monster metamorphosis. Snapping and clawing at the air around her like the truly tortured being she was, Lois blasted our kids for being kids. A fear of running into my mother, the bright lights, loud noises of a busy grocery store, and the constant touch, chatter, and gurgles from two little ones seemed to send my screaming nervous system beyond that one last frayed nerve.

In the aftermath, my husband took me aside and said, "You are terrifying our children. You are scaring me a bit, too, but you are *really* terrifying them!"

I yanked my arm and stomped away saying, "They are supposed to see what anger looks like!!!"

The Importance of Unravelling

In the lingering moment that the last word spit from my lip, I thought "Does my anger really teach them anything?" Fortunately, his words and this thought mingled with my defensive warrior body.

A couple of days later, Lois returned. My whole body flamed with her presence, head expanding, and cuss word vomit-exploding. The heat of her, this psycho bitch rage, burned pathways from my diaphragm straight up my torso. Waist, legs, feet like a huge boulder permanently grounded to the wooden dining room floor. Agitated arms flinched and flicked in spasms. Inside myself I heard the roar of her words. Streaks of light flashed. The walls of my body continued to roar as the blazing fire of her heat intensified. My face cooked with her furnace-blasted air. Brow deeply furrowed. Eyes squeezed into tiny slits seeing little as this rage, this Lois psycho bitch, blinded me in darkness. A roaring intake of breath; her blackened cloak over my face lifted. As the smoldering smog drifted upwards, I opened my eyes and looked.

My brain registered the faces, the little, beautiful, *terrified*, pale, saucer-eyed faces, staring, mouths frozen open, sitting, statues on the floor: my two children. Silence enveloped the room. No one breathed as I felt my heart pound. My face reddened with shame. I turned, stumbled into our bedroom with my hot pounding heart and head, flopped down onto our bed and sobbed uncontrollably into our cream-and-blue wedding ring quilt. I finally saw what my husband saw. My heart broke open. I called the next day for my first of many Cranio-Sacral appointments and sessions of Somatic Trauma Resolution. The passionate and rigorous journey of releasing Lois from my body, our home and our lives, forever, began.

Lois wasn't me, but an act, a front, a pretense, a grotesque inside-out costumed character. She raged with the F word; a word forbidden in my childhood home. For years she simmered with many flavors of fury deep in the lockdown pot of my body. She bubbled, vigorously boiled, and blew the lid right off especially in the early years of mothering my children. Lois splattered hurt all over these precious ones I treasured the most. Had I created her to cope? If I had, I succeeded in making one nasty creature.

Even though this psycho bitch rage, Lois, oddly fueled a distorted sense of courage for which I felt pride, I carried deep shame, too, realizing only cowards or deeply troubled people lash out at small beings. When you don't know the pathway out and you don't understand Post Traumatic Stress Disorder, reacting like a madwoman fools you into feeling powerful. Lois took over my body at the slightest provocation, when something in my immediate environment looked or smelled like a trigger from the past. I didn't invent her. She was my body screaming, *trauma lives right over here!*

The Importance of Unravelling

Out in the world with new people, different environments, and life experiences, I often perceived threats everywhere; I lost my ability to discern true danger from what only seemed dangerous. Anything that appeared remotely like the caldron of my childhood morphed into a threat. My system had automatically reacted mostly with freeze, of the fight, flight, freeze survival modalities. Now in a grownup body, I fought back, fueled by fury and the bottled-up hurt and anguish of all those years of numbly sucking it up. The fight response, while mostly unavailable in childhood inside the heinous dynamics of my parents' home and other so-called "safe havens," lived for years dormant inside of me.

Scenes from my past still visit me in moments when I'm in the shower, or running, and during times of quiet aloneness. These moments feel poignant as I honor all my courageous younger selves who endured persistent and heinous traumas. Waves of grief still come. Rather than pushing the sadness down inside of me, though, I allow the tears to fall. There remains much to grieve.

You may not have lived through trauma, yet you notice the waxy buildup of unresolved past hurts or heartbreaks. Maybe no one taught you how to deal with difficult emotions or experiences. Maybe you learned to bury your emotions, but they leak out sideways, unexpectedly. You might walk around ready to explode or you live disconnected, numb, anxious, lonely, or depressed. You go through the motions of living, very busy in your mind, but not really feeling your body, struggling to hear your heart. Barricading the hurt, you also wall off passion and joy. Emotionally flatlined in your fierce protection, you can barely breathe. You seek refuge in food, busyness, shopping, technology, and distractions of all kinds to avoid feeling or resolving anything.

Then another difficulty happens in present time that sets off an unravelling of all related past challenges that look and smell like the current one. Falling down a rabbit hole of DVR memories all opening up seemingly simultaneously takes you to your knees. Consciously choosing a different response in current time takes great courage because you see that you can no longer deny or avoid. In a ball of complete pain, you finally scream, "Uncle!" You know you must take the time to feel the shame, grief, rage, and hurt from all those past experiences. Feeling the emotional pain lodged in your heart and body becomes the price of your freedom.

The Importance of Unravelling

May you find safe ways to resolve past emotional hurts.
May you discover the joys, the freedom of healthy
emotional expression. May you know that you
are whole and well in your heart and soul.

The Death of Pretending

*"The world is his, who can see through its pretension …
see it to be a lie, and you have already dealt
it its mortal blow."*
—Ralph Waldo Emerson

Several years ago, my second husband and our two children and I lived where there was a large backyard and fenced deck next to a breezeway. On warm, sunny days, my children played in these spaces. One summer morning, we noticed a rancid smell that permeated the entire house. This putrid odor made all of us gag a bit. I had never smelled anything like this odor.

After investigating, my husband found a decomposing possum underneath the deck. Amazed that the pungent, indescribable odor could permeate our entire home from the outside, I felt grateful he had found the source. He wore a mask and struggled not to toss his cookies as he cleared away the remains.

I regularly share that the conditions of our spaces are metaphors for our lives. I know signs come in all kinds of packages, sometimes nasty ones. I looked up possum in my Power Animal book. These creatures pretend to be dead as a coping strategy. Predators want live possum. The scavengers and decomposers obviously relish the dead ones.

I laughed as I read this. When I reflected on my life up to that moment, I realized I no longer needed to pretend about anything. Even though it took me years of bumbling along the path towards living true to myself, to living in greater alignment, I still sometimes notice I'm pretending about something. I'm better at catching this quickly as it often makes me irritable.

What are you pretending? Do you pretend to be sick when you are well? Do you pretend to be well when you are sick? Do you pretend to be in love when you are "meh"? Do you pretend to be happy, kind, blissful when you want to growl, snap, and roar? Do you pretend to be brave when you are petrified? Do you pretend you are poor when you are rich? Do you pretend to be rich when you have debts? Do you pretend that you are not addicted when you have a serious addiction? Do you pretend all is "fine" when all hell is breaking loose everywhere around you? Do you wait for others to tell you about your authenticity and have no clue what your genuine self feels like in your own body?

The Death of Pretending

The process of becoming yourself, of living true to your life purpose, takes time, practice, and focus. Becoming whole and integrated involves becoming vulnerable enough to tell the truth about what's going on inside of your heart, gut, soul, and your mind so you can begin to learn from your body.

Telling the truth to yourself can be such a brave step forward. Telling the truth that you discovered about yourself to others becomes an additional bold action. Being willing to hold a compassionate, safe space of non-judgment and listen deeply often allows others to reveal their heartfelt truths. Holding this sacred space can free others from pretending. What a profound gift your presence becomes for your colleagues and beloved ones. Living in a state of greater wholeness, alignment, and integration brings great joy.

May the death of pretending enter your life in a less noxious sign than a decomposing, stinking possum. May you honor the gift of your life by breathing fresh air and exhaling your honesty, your beauty, and your grace.

Dishwasher Running

*"Self-realization is the sweetest thing. It shows us how
we are fully responsible for ourselves, and that
is where we find our freedom."*
—Byron Katie

A couple of years after my second marriage ended, a wonderful man walked into my life. He's respectful of my hard-won independence and realizes that I can do many things on my own. I watched myself softening as I realized that he offers to help me because he's kind and enjoys being of service. I haven't been bristling too much at his helpfulness, even though I was used to doing things myself. But then there came that moment when he inadvertently tripped an old trigger.

After going on enjoyable dates, walking in parks, and even folding socks, we had brunch together sitting in my backyard. I had cooked our meal, and he offered to clean up. When I walked back into the kitchen, I noticed that the dishwasher was running.

I felt surprised as I noticed myself flare with angry thoughts: *Does he think I'm incompetent and unable to run my own dishwasher? Darn him. He stepped over the line! How dare he?* I quickly shifted into a deeper awareness of the old pattern of being emotionally belittled by my ex and the ways that had hurt. An old tape was running in my brain. I burst into tears. He walked back into the kitchen with my dog.

"I'm triggered, and first I want you to know how much I appreciate you cleaning up and running my dishwasher. And at first I was really angry that you thought I was incompetent and stupid because of old crap I had with my ex, and then I realized how bruised I am and don't ever want to be angry with you for being kind and doing thoughtful actions to support me. I own all of my hot mess right now. And mostly, thank you for cleaning up."

Tears continued streaming down my face as I felt a mixture of shame over my past and profound gratitude for this man looking at me with concern.

He gently approached me and put his hand on my arm. "Oh, hon. You can be angry with me."

I explained that I now know that being angry is a symptom and mostly not a feeling I experience much anymore. I shared that my initial anger covered up the hurt, shame, and pain I felt from my past. I told him I was determined to continue shifting to my deeper commitment to love him, rather than misinterpreting his actions through a worn-out filter.

"Well, I did the dishes and ran the dishwasher because it was full," he said. "I thought for a moment about asking you, but then decided it was part of cleaning up. And I don't want to walk on eggshells around you."

"Oh, I don't ever want you walking on eggshells around me, and that's why I'm sharing exactly what's happened inside of me just now. I love you. I care about you and love all the ways you care about me. Sometimes it overwhelms me, yet I know I can lean into this 'new normal.'"

He held me gently in his strong arms. My head nestled into his chest. He handed me a tissue from his pocket. I wiped my eyes and face.

Staying focused on the clean-up inside my internal world, what I like calling "my boat" of thoughts, feelings, body sensations, body movements, facial expressions, I find the greatest freedom. No longer concerned about other people, their words or reactions, I discover great peace in doing my work of living awake and as self-aware as possible. What a relief and an ongoing commitment to live empowered.

When you remain full of judgment about what other people are doing, saying or not doing, or not saying, you become distracted from your life commitments, your growth, healing, and the most important person in your life – you. Being your healthiest, most self-aware self can shift the quality of your interactions as you take full responsibility for your thoughts, feelings, words spoken, and deeds done. Having clarity about your commitments and values, you can shift to the one person you can heal and empower: you.

May you unravel your emotional reactions that are almost always connected to limited beliefs and past "training." May you cultivate compassion for yourself as you become aware of worn-out patterns that no longer support healthy interactions with those you love the most.

It Is Not Personal

"When you realize it's not personal, there is no longer a compulsion to react as if it were."
—Eckhart Tolle

After my daughter graduated from college and my son had relocated to California, I moved to North Carolina. I attended a women's entrepreneurial networking group that met once a month. I immediately experienced the facilitator's energy vibe of reactive dislike towards me, like a cat that hisses and swats with claws extended at your face.

"Hurry up, get in here, and sit down!" she hollered.

I hustled into the grocery store's breakout room of florescent lights. Twenty or so women seated in wooden chairs behind small tables arranged in a lopsided oval looked at me. One woman smiled at me and patted the empty chair next to her. Relieved, I sat down next to her. The facilitator welcomed and instructed us to pass business cards. She asked that we introduce ourselves one at a time. After the fifth woman shared her elevator speech, I raised my hand.

"May I ask a question?"

The facilitator looked at me with fierce, burning eyes.

"No, you may not!"

She then laughed, a cackling cruel laugh, as she turned her whole body, her full attention to the next woman, who was to stand and share her one-minute introduction. I watched the facilitator ask this woman questions, then invite other women to ask questions about her business. I took internal notes about her preferential treatment, her ways of interacting with the diverse group of female entrepreneurs.

The meeting concluded with an opportunity for anyone to share personal or professional experiences for which we were grateful. I bravely put my hand up. She called on me. I stood up and began sharing what I was grateful for. In mid-sentence, she harshly interrupted me.

"Sit Down! This is not the Academy Awards!"

My face blushed crimson as I quickly sat back down, humiliated in front of a group of women I was hoping to connect with professionally, if not personally. Her behavior towards me persisted at each monthly gathering. I chose to ignore her unkind behavior towards me because I managed to connect with some wonderful women who regularly showed up at this networking group.

However, after a year, I stopped attending. There had to be other places where I could be warmly welcomed. Enough was enough. I realized that this experience was no longer a good fit for me, for the experience of professional connections that I wanted to create in my life. Though I knew the facilitator's behavior towards me wasn't personal, my heart felt the lingering effects of public shaming. I recognized that familiar burn.

Intellectually, I have understood the idea that others' unkind words and deeds came out of those individuals. Yet, to be in a place of peace and wholeness, to fully see that what others did and said was never about me, became a holistic transformation that came in pieces, in gradual awakenings.

I finally let go of a limiting belief: *My imperfections or perceived imperfections are responsible for other people's anger towards me.* In this new reality, I recognize that: *There are no conditions when someone else's anger is about me or my perceived flaws or imperfections.* Their tone of voice, gestures, words, and actions are not mine. Period.

Maybe like me, some of you go through a stage, maybe many times of asking yourself: What did I do? Why did this happen? Do I need to turn myself into a pretzel or shape-shift into someone else to not have people act with such unkindness, anger, or criticism directed at me, especially when it seems chronic and maybe even unpredictable? Is it about my words, behaviors, or me?

To untangle and pull apart what is yours from what is someone else's can be very profound work. To be 100 percent clear about what is in your boat (internal world of beliefs, thoughts, and emotions, and then your actual words/behaviors) remains an important step. The best apology is changed behavior. To listen from a place of presence, to bear witness, and hold space for others in their boats can be quite a revealing and challenging ride down the stream.

May you find freedom in focusing on your internal world of thoughts and feelings, your words spoken, deeds done. I wish you the realization that you are only responsible for your words and deeds, even when others might demand that you clean up their messes.

In My Mind, My Dog Was Dying

"When we lose our tolerance for vulnerability, joy becomes foreboding."
—Brené Brown

Recently, in my new life in North Carolina, I experienced anticipatory grief for my dog. In my mind, I ran scared down a rabbit hole where my thoughts convinced me she was dying, my version of "foreboding joy," a conditioning towards the fear response in the midst of great joy in one's life. Living with stability, beauty, love, and grace these past several months in North Carolina has allowed tucked away fears to surface. As empowered as I've become, I'm not immune to anxieties and irrational thoughts.

Several months ago, Layla, my dog, had numerous teeth removed. The dental vet scared and shamed me about the horrible condition of her teeth and the periodontal disease that could eventually kill her. These comments stated so fiercely by an authority figure I had not ever met lodged themselves in my amygdala with sprouting tendrils of shamefear.

A few weeks ago, Layla began having tummy troubles. She had days here and there that she did not eat any food except maybe a biscuit with peanut butter. The very next day she'd eat again, resuming her normal routine. Every single time this happened, I experienced the grip of shamefear. I convinced myself that the tummy issues were related to the periodontal disease. The dental vet had strongly recommended the removal of all her teeth as the remedy, but that expense and surgery was not something I was willing to navigate. I felt shame about that, too.

Then in a week Layla did not eat for three of those days. My internal fears and shame persisted. All the past grief of losing three dogs, the resentment that there was no "pet financial support" when my marriage ended, and the shamefear that I hadn't done the right thing for Layla's health came pouring out of me in front of my significant other. He quietly held me in his arms as I heard the chain of thoughts/emotions I had linked together into this "it must be the truth" hot mess bundle. Both of my hands covered my tear-streaked face as he gently suggested that I could go to a new vet who would be kind, rather than fierce or shaming.

"You could choose to see what's happening with Layla right now. It might not have anything to do with her teeth," he offered.

Huh? That's a different thought. I realized I could face hard truths. I had felt shamefear a thousand times during my life journey. I could also face a truth that was not as awful as the "choking off life" one in my mind. My significant other recommended his vet. He promised that his veterinarian had a compassionate bedside manner mixed with gentle honesty and the ability to honor a pet owner's decisions.

I called for an appointment.

Layla felt so relaxed in this new vet's presence she lay down with her head curled to the side on top of the table immediately after he entered the patient room. The new vet showed me that her remaining teeth and gums are healthy. He and his staff did some testing for heartworm and Lyme disease, which all came out negative. They also did a procedure that helps many dogs with what seems like a digestive issue. Since this appointment, Layla's been happily eating, eliminating, wiggling, barking with joy, and sleeping peacefully at night.

The rigorous work of pulling apart the messes of the past from a current, sometimes much more benign challenge continues to be my path, an uncomfortable, yet ultimately liberating journey. Freed for this moment from old fears, I laughed at myself with relief, gratitude, and joy.

Being an emotionally and mentally healthy human can be a long walk of humility, vulnerability, and courage.

May you courageously unravel past experiences that might be clouding current realities. May you see this moment with clear eyes, a quiet mind, and a loving heart, and respond with compassion for yourself and others.

Lost My Voice, Found Myself, Again

"Difficulties come when you don't pay attention to life's whisper. Life always whispers to you first, but if you ignore the whisper, sooner or later you'll get a scream."
—Oprah Winfrey

Living in the mountains of North Carolina on a Thanksgiving holiday weekend I lost my voice. Laryngitis wrapped its red swollen, cracked fingers around my vocal cords. Talking created discomfort. I muted myself to heal. As someone who loves to express herself with spoken words, I found gratitude and rich lessons inside the silence, once again.

I often take advantage of body ailments as a time to be curious about the mental, emotional, relational, and contextual conditions of my life. I broaden my view to all these areas because I've learned that repeated, familiar body ailments often connect to limiting beliefs that linger like that last bit of dog poo that I cannot scrape off my shoe after stepping, again, in a pile. The ailment almost always connects to unresolved feelings that haven't fully processed through my heart.

I look at "pay attention to me!" body issues as a window to the rest of my life, a process I have been doing for years to great benefit.

This holistic perspective honors the mind/body/emotion connection because I know I'm not an isolated clump of symptoms. I'm an entire human being connected to the people I care about, the thoughts I think, the feelings that flow, and the past I lived. I also know that I can watch all of this from my ever-quiet internal witness.

A couple of weeks ago, the man I hired to create *Cherish Your World* videos had set up all his equipment outside on his driveway. As the temperature rapidly dropped here in the mountains, the winds picked up ferociously creating a biting wind chill. I had texted him earlier to request that "Maybe we tape inside today." However, he believed that shooting outside would stay consistent with the other footage of excerpts from *Let Go Courageously*. A handful of chapters remained to be read.

Thinking he would honor my request to remain inside, I arrived in skinny jeans, hiking boots, a fleece jacket over a cotton sweater with no hat, scarf, or gloves. A metal stool awaited my bony bottom. Speaking up did not even occur to me. A lifelong pattern of automatically acquiescing to what seems like an authority figure, a person who appears to "know better than I do" took over my whole way of being. Days later, I revisited this moment over and over again wanting to understand and dismantle an unhealthy habituated reaction.

I climbed up on the cold metal stool, followed his cues, and began reading the last chapters of my book. The icy wind gusts began to take my breath away as my body shivered with cold. We took breaks to warm up inside his house. He noted that the wind chill had plummeted into the teens. He offered me gloves, a hat, a thicker coat that I layered on top of my fleece, which did little to warm my already bone-chilled body. We powered forward. I could no longer bear siting on the icy metal stool. I stood shivering as I read the final two chapters. How did my voice not quiver?

I drove away in full body shakes, teeth chattering, the heat blasting from my car, my hands like icy tentacles attempting to grip the steering wheel. I couldn't remember ever feeling this cold. The brilliant sunshine could not warm anything. All I could focus on was getting home to a hot shower and sipping hot cups of tea.

I don't know about you, but I own that I got trained from a very young age to step into grownup shoes, to take on more than I was designed to endure, and to "suck it up." A mantra delivered loudly and clearly during my childhood came through: "When the going gets tough, the tough get going." I wanted to be a "tough" one, even though so much of who I am at my core remains tender and sensitive. The demand for the yang of masculine energy in an unbalanced, unhealthy expression became and still becomes a way to cope, to survive, to produce results in a world that seemed to demand that I earn my right to exist.

The act of sitting on a metal stool in the freezing cold didn't seem like a big deal given my past training. And yet, wow, really?

I acknowledge that a healthy, centered response to the videographer could have been to say, "I honor that you'd like the footage to be outside and consistent because you have an excellent eye for what creates an inviting video. I also appreciate that you've got everything set up. However, I am not willing to sit in the freezing cold. I don't have that bandwidth or the proper clothing. Let's reschedule for when the weather is warmer."

As I live with the natural consequences of not taking care of my body like I could have, I'm grateful for another opportunity to shed limiting beliefs and those feelings of powerlessness that a young child or even a grown adult can experience. As I listen first to my body's wisdom, to my freezing self after that shoot, to my currently inflamed vocal cords, and my heart's compassion, I can retrain my mind.

Before the laryngitis fully set in, I called the videographer. I created a break in our work together as

I knew I needed to allow these learnings to settle in, and the holidays had him very busy. I took full responsibility for silencing my voice that day and regretted doing so. He apologized when he realized he could have been more patient in waiting for another warm day. We realized there was rich learning for both of us.

Some of us might get to hike many times around the mountain, living and reliving certain pieces and parts of experiences until the layers of lessons finally sink all the way down to our chilled-to-the-bone bones. Maybe next time we'll advocate powerfully and confidently for ourselves without hesitation. At the very least, we could pause to listen for our body's truth, for what yearns to be expressed. Or maybe we'll simply show up in the proper gear.

Have you noticed how familiar challenges continue to cycle through your life that present opportunities to do the deeper dive of healing from a place of greater safety, understanding, and compassion?

Have you ever powered through a situation without even thinking about the harm you were doing to your body, your psyche, your heart, or your relationships?

How many times have you not spoken up to authority figures? How many times when you did speak up to authority figures were you not heard or believed? How many times did your speaking the truth or pushing back create a ripple of backlashes that robbed you of your freedom, dignity, or sense of self-empowerment?

May you bravely relinquish ways of being in your life that no longer support you. May you create fresh responses to people and life events because your unique perspective matters. May you experience self-empowerment.

Exoskeleton

At first glance you scare me.
Like a terrifying image of the past
With sharp edges, pinchers, and maybe a hidden sting.
The packaging of you remains stunningly intact.
From this exterior view you look like you.

With closer curious inspection
You are only the outer design
I could flick away,
Or with a breeze of wind
You'd blow away light as the feather you now are,
A ghost town of memories.

Every day I awake and
Squiggle away from you.
You hold a past that is no longer who I am or ever was.
I thank you for being the container
For holding space for the very essence of me.

I have crawled out,
Flown into the trees
Free to sing and mate.

For now I have found safe haven,
Home in the depths of an inner world
Filled with equanimity, peace, acceptance
Dense with love
Here in the woods of my soul.

SECTION TWO

Living True

The Voice of Courage

Your toddler girl body and best friend's girl body
soiled at the hands and threats of a stranger.
Balled in terror I coaxed you
To barely breathe
A begging mantra
"We won't tell. Let us live."

Waking up terrified at night
I whispered, "You are alive."

Hidden deep inside, I helped your
Body move, hide, and comply in a
Household where
Eggshell walking
Required calloused feet
You did not have.

Looking into your brown eyes
In that reflection of mirrored glass
I said, "We will get out of here."

We began digging underground
Passageways inside your imagination
and fluttering heart
To find escape.

You skated, swam, and ran.
Your body grew and so did I.
We began to speak and take the heat.
I found a place inside your vocal cords.
"Use your words." I said.

No one hears your truth.
I feel absent in the ears of others.
Cowardice makes people deaf
With disbelief.

You and I hold hands with dark truths.
We hold our breath
Curl our toes,
Clench our jaw,
Freeze our eyes,
until

We know it's safe to exhale the pain
Purge the nastiness
Scribble out the rage of hurt.

Sword down the back
A beautiful green dress,
Fingers and thumb poised to curl into
Balls with a forceful erection.
Stone cold eyes
Fists pumping air
Bursting out the most forbidden words
Of All.
I now embody you as a profane warrior.

Talk down your pounding fierceness.
Unfurl your voice of wounded rage.
Soften and relinquish this protective stance.
Drop the sword, fall on your knees,
Weep an ocean of tears
Coiled underneath that waterfall of hurts.

"Find stillness. Find the silence," I said.
Beneath the surface of water
Holding your breath

Yet breathing deeply,
You find me in the quiet of your heart,
In the intersection of your grief and joy.

You begin to see me in the eyes of beloved ones
Who actually love you, hear you
Who hold your hands
Who look at you, celebrate you
Accept you in all ways.

"Soften in the arms of love."
I say.
For Love and I are One.

Courage at the Core

Be brave. Without bravery, you will never know the world as richly as it longs to be known. Without bravery, your life will remain small – far smaller than you probably wanted your life to be."
—*Elizabeth Gilbert*

When I began graduate school at The Ohio State University, I joined three other women in my class. I received two distinguished scholarships along with the opportunity to work as a professor's assistant, which I gratefully accepted. Surrounded by an all-male faculty and mostly male classmates, I knew I'd need my courage.

A diligent, bright student from years of disciplined practice, I entered grad school married to my first husband. I had work experience. I quickly learned that all my classmates came directly from undergraduate school. Having a home to care for, a husband, and a cat, I seemed like a Muggle who had walked into Hogwarts. I quickly learned that my worldly realities remained oddities. Most professors and students turned their lives completely over to the cloistered world of the ivory towers.

One professor lived on campus in a dorm for easy access to his office during the many times he worked through the night. When I entered his office a few minutes late for an appointment because I had been delayed at a veterinarian's visit with the cat, he looked at me perplexed like an alien who dared have a life beyond books. He questioned my commitment to the program, to my studies. I was never late to another appointment with him.

Then there was the class on the U.S. Congress that I attended. Taught by an esteemed faculty member who had been wooed to OSU from another elite university, the course quickly became my least favorite.

The professor embodied those pompous ways that annoyed me. I sat in his classroom disgruntled and unmotivated. I had interacted with all types of men up to this point in my life including smart, kind men, Good Ole Boys, Ladies Men, misogynists, and pathological predators. Before entering grad school, I had worked in the Ohio State Legislature as an intern.

During the first week, he asked us who made up our U.S. Congress. I raised my hand. He called on me. I said, "Old. White. Men."

He shot back, "What's wrong with old, white men? I'm an old, white man!" I silently looked at him.

I met privately with this professor after I received my first "failing" grade, a B-, on a mid-term exam in his class. He looked at me over his rimmed glasses from behind his large wooden desk.

"I really don't understand why you are here in this program. You're married. You're just going to get pregnant. You'll end up leaving the program to mother your babies. Why would we waste our time investing in you, dear? You're just a woman."

He obviously had not been on the admissions committee because I might have had to change my name to Larry instead of Laura.

He knew almost nothing about me. I chose to take his disbelief in my intellect, my wholeness as a person, to fuel my already honed work ethic. Thankfully, I did not have to take another course from him. I earned my MA, divorced my husband because it wasn't a healthy marriage, moved back to my hometown, passed General Exams, and earned a position as a part-time faculty member at Ohio Wesleyan University, where I taught for five years, while I completed my dissertation.

Working with my supportive committee members at OSU, I researched, wrote, and defended a solid dissertation. The major findings matched a report by a national women's organization on national trends in women's success in winning public office and the numbers of women stepping into the political arena. I had found the same pattern on the local level over a three-decade period.

I walked across the stage, received my doctoral hood from my dad, was embraced by my advisor, and handed a Ph.D. by the provost of The Ohio State University. I told many friends and family that my second husband and I would celebrate, that I'd become pregnant. God or Someone heard me because nine months later I gave birth to my daughter. With the support of my husband, I chose to be a fulltime parent as a calling of my heart and soul at a time when my peers quickly returned to paying jobs after giving birth. Becoming an emotionally healthy, loving, conscientious, and skilled parent became its own beautiful, challenging transformative journey. Years later I threw out all of my graduate school papers in a brave clutter-clearing when I knew that I'd never return to the classroom as an academic.

I have never regretted anything I've bravely done in my life. I've learned that a life lived in terror or chronic high anxiety is not a life worth living. While it would be wonderful for my two adult children to be happy, I also fiercely want them to live with courage in their hearts that overflows into their words and deeds and grows strong inside their souls.

Courage at the Core

Courage infused with values lives at the very core of what drives a meaningful life. Can you think of any important advancements towards an aspiration, micromovements towards fulfillment, or an awakening in your life that didn't take courage?

To speak the truth to a domineering person, to do the right thing on behalf of those who may feel powerless, to see an enemy as a human being takes courage. To share mistakes and failures vulnerably with shame and remorse among those who may not hear you, to suppress a giggle when everyone around you is crying, to weep when many around you are chuckling, to remain silent when all you want to do is yell "F#$% You!!" requires discipline, discernment, and courage.

Bravery fuels showing up for life when you might want to stay under the covers. To choose to move outside your comfort zone, to confront your own inner critic with the truth of who you really are and why you are here requires courage. To stand alone, to walk away, to run towards your deepest dreams and desires for a life filled with freedom often demands a brave commitment. Courage exists as an essential ingredient for growth, development, differentiation, and self-actualization.

Living inside this daring can be messy and uncomfortable because you probably will trip and fall in the mud as you walk away from what no longer supports or inspires you. After taking a moment to laugh at yourself, I hope you will keep walking. Brave actions create intended and unintended results for which you are fortunate to be responsible. You will feel very much alive.

May most people you encounter experience your gifts, love, compassion, humor, and strength. May you know that these qualities all came from a fierce, unrelenting willingness to live bravely. May you be fiercely brave for your heart-centered dreams no matter what others think or say. May your courage open doors to a more joyful experience of loving your beautiful, precious life.

Pay Attention to the Truth

"It's helpful to think of lying as a defiance of the truth and BS-ing as a wholesale dismissal of the truth."
—Brené Brown

At fourteen years old while attending a summer church camp, I witnessed my tentmate being raped by our male counselor. When I saw her black, round, saucer eyes, and pale-white, terrified face that still burns in my brain to this day, I urged her to tell someone.

"If you don't tell, I will."

I held her hands. She remained silent.

I told.

The next day a man that I had not ever encountered during my time at the camp approached me. He took me out in a boat on the lake. Insisting that nothing had happened, he declared that I had had a great experience at camp, that I would tell my parents I had a wonderful time.

He added that besides, if this had actually happened, my counselor would get fired.

"You like your counselor, don't you?! You wouldn't want him to be fired. He's worked really hard. It would be your fault if he were fired."

At this juncture, I chose silence. Having persistently navigated much worse situations, I knew when to become silent.

This man in the boat did a brilliant job of both threatening and BS-ing. He attempted to convince me that nothing had happened, which was a wholesale dismissal of the truth. He, at the same time, alluded to some acceptance that the rape could have happened by threatening me with being held responsible for the counselor's probable firing. When people refuse to see hard truths, interactions become quite challenging.

Having grown up in a chaotic, shapeshifting, confusing world filled with tortured adults who regularly lied or dismissed the truth, I discovered that finding solid ground inside my intuition and lived experiences was invaluable. I often knew those adults were angry, even though they claimed to be joking. Though I'd also get confused when they dismissed or denied my reality, my body registered the truth of what I lived and observed. Now, as an adult, I fairly quickly discern when something's "off" with a person, an interaction, or a situation. My difficult childhood "training"

Pay Attention to the Truth

serves me, especially when others may not initially see, feel, or notice what I do.

When a truth is known, yet denied, then dismissed as nonexistent, a commitment to the facts becomes an act of courage, integrity, and authenticity.

You know you're in a hot mess when people are having arguments about whether the ketchup bottle on the table is a mug of coffee or a bag of potato chips. You also know you've entered a challenging situation when you walk into a room and see that others do not feel safe to ask questions, to be curious, to offer a fresh perspective or a commonsense way of seeing things. If individuals feel threatened and consumed with fear, finding pathways to the truth becomes quite arduous.

When fear lives in the underbelly of the conversation, it will be difficult to find common ground on some basic realities. The best you may be able to do is to say, "Fear is palpable in this room. It's distorting our ability to see or hear one another. To what are we committed? What needs to be resolved that's in the backdrop? How are we framing the discussion?"

When words start flying around that contradict each other, when those same words consistently don't match behaviors, or when questions enter your mind because you latched onto both the lies and the BS, then these become the moments to pause. Heightened emotions often block pathways to rational thinking. Neuroscience shows that fear and the fight, flight, and freeze reactions shut down access to the prefrontal cortex, the reasoning part of the brain.

Deep breathing from the diaphragm, placing the tongue on the roof of the mouth, opening the mouth slightly, standing up with dignity in the spine, bending the knees slightly, softening the eyes, relaxing the arms by your side all guide your body to a more neutral, calmer place. These body movements can interrupt a highly charged interaction. The body can lead the way, and the mind can learn a new pattern. Shifting to a neutral place, a pause immediately after something happens, opens up a world of possible responses. A response can flow from a place of deeper commitment and be a reflection of your core values.

Continuing to strengthen the part of you that can hold space, that can be a detached observer of you, that can watch the movie of your thoughts and feelings while committing to a deeper place of quiet, allows you to hear the strong emotions and words of others. This expanded awareness creates opportunities to choose from many possible responses including bravely speaking the truth of your lived experiences and your observations. Sometimes you must be willing to set aside your need to belong for the truth to emerge. And just because people may not believe you does not mean difficult things didn't happen. Their BS-

Pay Attention to the Truth

ing does not alter reality. To be committed to your integrity and authenticity, you must be very brave indeed. It takes courage to hear, believe, and speak hard truths.

*May you courageously speak difficult truths.
May these truths free you.*

Perceptions of Others

*"No one can make you feel inferior
without your consent."*
—*Eleanor Roosevelt*

A while ago, a dear friend in my network let me know that he saw me as a visionary for *Cherish Your World*. I was touched by this inspiring perception of me, so I shared his feedback with a different friend. She fiercely advised me not to include this word in anything I said or wrote about myself because she felt it to be bragging. Her words: "If others say this about you, that's fine, but don't you *dare* say it about yourself." I heeded her advice.

Just recently, two very close friends let me know that I'm really smart and intuitive, but sometimes I come off as emotional. They invited me to keep integrating my intellect with my intuition and emotions.

Their advice made sense to me because I do cry easily, so most likely I am sometimes perceived as soft with no backbone or little intellect, even though this remains far from the reality of who I am.

I sometimes openly get teary-eyed with a mix of grief and gratitude in front of others, including people I've only recently met. Knowing my whole life that public crying is definitely not cool has not made a great deal of difference to my heart and eyes. I accept that I have a tender heart and leave others to deal with their discomfort.

In my past, I learned to shroud my intelligence. Being a smart young woman was not popular. I noticed in different settings when I shared insights about our political world or football, I got asked when I was getting married and having children. Even today, I can see how others may not know I earned higher degrees and that I really am bright. I also know intellect means little if I am unable to apply the learnings to life situations.

Who we turn to for honest feedback matters on our journey to know ourselves, to own our lives, and to create unique ways to make a positive difference for other people. Sometimes trusted others' perceptions and experiences of us light the way. At other times, people project their own pain, expectations, or limited beliefs onto us. Learning to sift through what might be useful to our growth, grabbing the treasures, and dumping out the rest can be quite a process. People seem to love to share opinions, solicited and unsolicited with others. Add another soundtrack

Perceptions of Others

called "the thoughts in our mind," and it is no wonder that we end up a bit confused about who we really are and what we are supposed to do with our lives.

Examining what you don't know that you don't know about yourself requires willingness, curiosity, and courage. You may walk around with misperceptions of yourself and others can show up as seers. Individuals who actually have your back and want you to be fulfilled can often offer sound, meaningful insights.

Sometimes you easily see other people's blind spots, but not your own. Alternatively, you quickly see the best in other people, excuse or even deny their foibles, painfully notice your own flaws and imperfections, and downplay your strengths and gifts. Occasionally, you meet people who tell you they are perfect exactly the way they are, and you wonder whether this could even be possible or if this has become their masterfully crafted pretense.

When those connected to you see your goodness and the parts of your "work in progress," you have a richer picture of yourself. From this place you can filter their input with your own inner awareness to see if their comments resonate with your heart. Finding that quiet place of bearing witness supports the process of releasing limiting beliefs and embracing the deeper truths of who you are. You can then hear others' feedback and your own thoughts as possible truths. More importantly, you can choose what you create, what actions you take, and what you give to our world.

May you listen to those who genuinely want the best for you. May you offer your honest feedback as a contribution to those who ask you. May you come to know yourself as fully and completely as possible.

Breaking Free

*"Shame corrodes the very part of us that
believes we are capable of change."*
— Brené Brown

Several years ago, I spent a hot afternoon with my two young children at the zoo. They rode in a wooden Red Flyer wagon during most of our visit. We loved seeing the animals, but some people became a challenge to observe. As we walked through the exit gates, I noticed a woman surrounded by children. She was drinking from one of those supersized cups they sell at the zoo and many amusement parks. A little boy, who only came up to her knees, kept reaching up. I assumed he was her son. He cried, wanting a sip of her beverage. She hit him hard across the face and roared angry words at him. He flinched, and cried harder, but remained undaunted in his pleas for a drink. His arms continued to stretch towards the cup. She roared and hit him hard again.

I stopped. At a safe distance I yelled, "Can I help you?"

She roared at me, "CAN YOU FUCKING HELP ME?!?!"

"Yes, can I help you?"

"CAN YOU FUCKING HELP ME?"

I observed that she had stopped striking the little boy's head. She had turned full-on towards me. Sweat trickled down my back. My sunglasses felt very hot on my face. The heat from the sun seemed to have intensified. I remained motionless.

"Yes, Because I know what it's like to be that angry!!"

She roared, "YOU KNOW WHAT IT'S LIKE TO BE THIS ANGRY!"

"Yes, I do."

She was me. I was her. Behind closed doors, I had been the little boy too.

I then turned towards my children. She continued to roar these words at my back as I pulled the wagon through the exit.

I spoke to my children. "Some adults are hurting inside. It's not okay for them to hit their children. She has a lot of anger inside her body. Children are not for hurting."

Both of them nodded at me with wide eyes. I could not shield my children from witnessing violence towards other children. I painfully remembered the one-time private striking of my own daughter on her bottom when I was enraged as well as other shame-filled moments of yelling. I, thankfully, had begun my deep work with gifted therapists to heal my past traumas, and the ways in which I had done my private version of anger episodes with my really young children.

As I drove by the exit area, I saw the woman sitting, leaning against a wall in some shade with the children sitting around her. The little boy held the supersized cup. The woman's face and whole body had shifted into a picture of crestfallen, exhausted defeat. I felt my heart clench. Internal words channeled through me from beyond my mind when I looked out my vehicle window at her.

A silent prayer for her healing and my own. A fervent mantra for the life of that little boy. "May you find peace. God is love. God is love. May you find peace."

A chill tingled through my body. Goosebumps appeared on my arms. The witness, a courageous voice for lifting the shame, interrupting the behavior, awakening a new possible pathway for her and for me emerged.

Did that little boy become a grown man filled with the corrosion of shame, limited in his ability to change, to break free?

I now understand why toxic words and behaviors from tortured, unhealed people can be so daunting to overcome for children and adults. Pained others' ability to pour out and twist shame into something that now seems like yours can be quite stunning. To the extent you ingest the poisonous words of another that are not aligned with your deepest truths, you become a shame container, a body filled with other people's projected nastiness mixed with your own mistakes. The grain of truth in what is spoken can become the catalyst for change.

Some of you may have heard the story of the monk walking with his student. A stranger approaches the monk. This unknown person taunts the monk for several miles of the walk. The monk never responds. Finally, the stranger walks away. The student, puzzled that the monk never reacted in anger or defense, asks him, "Why did you not react? The monk looks at the student. "When someone gives you a gift and you do not accept it, who does the gift belong to?"

Pulling apart another person's pontificating words and actions from your deeper truths can become a lifetime process if you've had many unkind words spoken to you or hurtful deeds done by others including parents, bosses, teachers, principals, schoolyard bullies, or even people you thought were your friends. This process can become enduring work to see who you really are, to grow, and transmute the shaming words and deeds of others. These limiting, demeaning beliefs likely became your inner critic. The shame belongs to all those other people, not inside of you. That pearl of your beautiful humanity knows your own spoken words and deeds. The round whitish-pink tiny sea jewels remain firm, strong, resilient, and beautiful.

May you breathe, pause, feel your heart's truth before you speak and bravely walk towards your dreams, your most fulfilling life. May you collect oysters, prying them open to discover those pearls that formed from a healing coating around the grit of negative experiences. May these beauties shine in the palm of your hand, affirming the natural creation that is your glistening life.

The Dance of Trust and Discernment

"When something feels off, it is."
—Abraham Hicks

After becoming an independent, single woman with grown children and choosing to be a full-time entrepreneur, I drove one morning to a business networking event at the local Costco in central Ohio. Feeling a bit of confidence, I extended my hand to the first person I saw. He shared that he was a financial advisor. We struck up a conversation in which he asked intriguing questions that led me to believe he was interested in *Cherish Your World* and how I help people. Still struggling with a certain amount of naïveté about people's agendas and feeling tender in my recent singlehood, I noticed how handsome and charming he was. I felt an energy vibe between us that blurred the line between professional and personal. The

Happily Flattered Florence part of me was being noticed, seen, and appreciated. I hadn't felt that feeling in years.

Later that day I received a charming message through LinkedIn asking if we could meet for coffee. Again, the language blurred the line. The Florence part of me took over. The financial advisor and I met. He continued with many charming ways that had I been savvy, not so emotionally thirsty, I would have thrown many flags on the play. He revealed enough about himself and his life to seem trustworthy. I realize as I look back that this was part of his business seduction game. I allowed myself to be played like a fiddle.

At one point he told me I needed to be 100 percent transparent. Well, that was easy as I openly shared about my financial situation. At one point, I burst into tears, excused myself to go to the restroom to pull myself together. Talking about money matters felt like getting naked with my shame and unworthiness, especially after having lived through a terrifying contested divorce in which my ex bullied me every step of the way. Talking about this experience to the financial advisor, I revealed raw, unfiltered thoughts and feelings. He got me right where he wanted me by making several promises about my money that sounded legitimate and intelligent. He failed to be fully transparent with me.

Trusting his words and ignoring my gut, I transferred a Roth IRA over to his company.

A year later when I chose to work with a different, trustworthy financial advisor I learned that had I died during that year time period; the other advisor's company would have gotten all the money in the Roth IRA instead of my two children. With this new knowledge, I transferred the Roth IRA back to the established financial institution in which the monies had originally been placed. I took this action at great financial cost, but it was worth my peace of mind. I experienced another painful life lesson about my own gullibility and vulnerability.

When shaming, fear tactics, or flattery flow into the mix of business, I place myself on high guard. Painful experiences allow me to be much better at listening to my gut and pausing before I make an important choice. I know not to do business when I'm raw, emotionally hungry, or not feeling centered. Unscrupulous people come in all kinds of packages. Paying attention from a centered place is an important practice.

To me, trust means the ability to count on people to show up fairly consistently as who they claim to be. Likely you have challenging moments that cause you to react, sometimes badly, but with self-accountability, remorseful apology, and course correction, you can get back on track with being consistent and trustworthy. Your character qualities cannot be trained into or imposed on you. Your energy essence travels with you.

Yet what happens when things don't work or work intermittently, people seem different than you expect, and something seems off-kilter? You might get confused. You realize you need to learn to trust yourself. Discernment enters the dance as a healthy partner to trust. You increase your ability to discern truth from lies, reality from pretense, your gut reactions from your sometimes overriding "be polite" thoughts, and the subtle nuances along a continuum of human behaviors. Sometimes the betrayal of trust is crystal clear, and sometimes betrayals sneak in the backdoor.

How you respond when life goes wonky and people betray your trust reveals a new type of trust, an inner knowing that you can handle the situation, be resilient, and maybe even respond with greater clarity. The contrasts show up as indicators of your ability to pay attention and choose differently. Wonky days can lead to more stable ones as you learn to shift internally, to take wiser, aligned actions.

Trust and discernment live inside of you. Cultivating the ability to listen to your intuition and heart's whispers from a grounded place might take years of practice and painful lessons. Walking away from what isn't good for you and towards what is exquisitely wonderful for your life takes courage because you're likely dismantling past training. No matter what happens, your inner guidance system will always cue you.

May you listen to your gut instincts, because the body does not ever lie. May you expand your ability to trust yourself and discern truths in your life. May you dance with all that life brings.

The Practice of Patience

"Patience is not simply the ability to wait – it's how we behave while we're waiting."
—Joyce Meyer

While waiting for family and friends to arrive at our house, I placed some toys in the living room for my two-year-old daughter to play with. This kept her engaged as I did final tasks to prepare our home for guests. Knowing my daughter, I felt confident she would gravitate to and be mesmerized by the yellow shape-sorter with the blue lid, a new learning toy. I saw that I was correct, which gave me the opportunity to work close by in the kitchen.

A few months earlier, my daughter had learned to pick up small pieces of food on the tray of her high chair by placing the pinkie side of her small right hand next to the morsel, then gently squeezing her hand into a fist around the piece of food to help it slide to the top of that opening formed by her curled pointer finger and thumb. Then, with her fist crowned by a piece of food, she'd take it to her mouth. Feeding herself in this unique way delighted me; it still does even now as I vividly recall her process. Eventually, she discovered her opposable thumbs and the ability to grasp food between pointer finger and thumb.

The doorbell rang. Our guests arrived. My daughter remained engrossed in feeling the shapes and attempting to place them in the yellow cylinder container. I invited family and friends inside, hung up coats, and offered beverages and snacks, which were in the kitchen. The adults greeted one another while my daughter remained happily focused on her toy. She tried over and over again, unsuccessfully, to get a shape into a matched slot.

All of a sudden, an important adult in her life reentered the room, noticed her "struggle," walked over, opened the lid, grabbed the shapes out of her hands, threw them into the yellow container, and slammed the blue lid. I didn't say a word. My daughter looked at him, perplexed. I wouldn't have described this adult as a patient person. He also wasn't teaching or guiding. He seemed to grow agitated with her learning curve, like he couldn't bear her process for one more moment. I assumed he held a short bandwidth for a toddler's way or at least my daughter's, in this instance.

His actions might be like people around you or you may interrupt other individuals' learning process. Rather than ask if you can help or allow the person time to figure out a puzzle, you may step in to take over. Learning something new can take time and involve many missed shots at the basket or strikeouts.

Do you have the patience to persist in your learning? Can you hold space in silence and stillness while others do their searching? Why do we sometimes impulsively insert ourselves into someone else's learning process? Is rescue actually about help or impatience?

I realize I live in a fast-paced, get the answer right now, immediate reply to email, "You should know this by now!" earn-a-million-dollars-overnight kind of world. Experience shows me that patience and learning over time, while making many mistakes, has sustainable benefits.

Some of you may notice you lack the bandwidth for patience. You expect or demand instant learning within yourself and from others. Some of you are fast learners; there's hardly a curve in your learning. You might assume everyone else is wired for that fast track, "AHA, I got it!" like you are. Maybe you have natural proclivities and innate talents that come into play with this too. Learning something new that excites and interests you can become an unstoppable train of curiosity that navigates countless obstacles for a lifetime.

On the other hand, you may be someone who must take time to ponder, to process, to integrate, to practice a new idea or skill. Reflecting, ruminating, wondering, and wandering are important to your learning and growing process. You do not approach things like a firestorm or a big "whoosh," but rather like a slow, often quiet in the background, analytical way. You likely think through many possibilities or "kick lots of tires" before you take action. You are the opposite of impulsive in a world that seems to demand "Right Now!" However, your quieter, more intuitive, less flashy introverted ways often result in astonishingly meaningful, enduring contributions.

Likely the interplay among the rush from experiences or immediate actions, thoughtful introspection, and the deliberate, meaningful integration and application of recent learnings allow patience to serve as a foundation of your process as all these are important for growth.

You can experience delicious freedom when you realize not everyone else has to do things like you do or in the timeframe you desire. Pondering a question, taking actions, having experiences, integrating the fresh insights for days, weeks, or years create integrated fresh perspectives, and sometimes a new life trajectory. Percolating can result in a delicious cup of coffee and a sustainable, opened, unlimited view of life's possibilities. Some learnings are supposed to take time and require the deep, long breath of patience.

The Practice of Patience

May you find the flow among action, introspection, and deliberate application in your learning process. May you allow others to learn new skills in their time and their way. May you discover patience as a refreshing practice, a way to live your life.

The Courage to Be You

*"It takes courage to show up and
become who you really are."*
—e. e. cummings

With much love and care, my brother and sister-in-law delivered a fried chicken dinner days after our second child was born. I felt so grateful for this hot meal. Breastfeeding my infant son created a hunger like no other. I began eating every single bite of food on my loaded plate: the mashed potatoes, gravy, corn on the cob, and chicken complete with the delicious crunchy, greasy skin. I even drooled a bit.

A former neighbor stopped by with a vegan baby cake. She sat down as we were eating and began fiercely delivering a lecture about the evils of ingesting chicken, the cruel ways chickens are slaughtered, and on and on. What she didn't realize was that as a breastfeeding mom, the bonding hormone, oxytocin, flowed freely through my body, so much so that I barely heard her words or felt her judgment. The situation was actually quite comical. I almost laughed out loud.

Thank goodness I had some sense to take her as seriously as I could. It's not that I didn't respect her cause or appreciate the truth of what she was saying, but if she was trying to bring me along as a convert, she failed utterly. I made a promise to myself not ever to evangelize about the evils of anything – especially not to a breastfeeding mom of a newborn baby.

I also remember an experience a few years ago. Soon after I created my company as a fulltime adventure, I received a call from a woman insisting I alter my makeup for an optimal professional look. She had met me in person earlier that day at a networking meeting. While I intuitively knew I needed to purchase new facial products (what woman doesn't?), I immediately felt her criticism. Her "tsk tsk" about my current look crackled through the phone line. My ears and cheeks burned with shame. The doorbell rang, so I finally spoke.

"My doorbell just rang. There are people here to fix pipes in my house. I had a sewage back-up this past weekend."

I thanked her for reaching out, laughed nervously when I told her the contractors had top priority in my life, and we ended the call. I made an internal note to get a makeover at some later date and not ever hire her for assistance.

In both these situations, the women failed to note the context in which they were calling or visiting. So wrapped up inside their own agendas, they failed to connect from the heart with care or a meaningful, thoughtful question about me, my life, or my family.

I forgive them, for I've done the same.

Someone could be blogging about their experiences of me as one self-absorbed, fear-driven person. Another woman could be writing right now about my failure to connect that happened a couple of weeks ago. In a moment of anxiety, I had approached her. We had never met, but I had overheard her saying something about clearing clutter. I swooped in with a flyer about an upcoming workshop I was facilitating. Fear. Agenda-driven. My hands shook. She stared at me, politely took the flyer, asked who I was, then turned and walked away. I ran after her and profusely apologized for my brashness. I can still bumble.

What a painful reminder that coming from fear-driven agendas remains a bankrupt way to connect with others, let alone to be of service or support people.

You may have had similar experiences of being judged for making different choices or see yourself as a fear-driven carrier of someone else's script. Transcending these survival modalities takes focus and resilience.

Can you imagine a world where we all began conversations from settled silence rather than fear, from presence rather than breathless agendas, from a place of openness and curiosity?

I imagine that the person you aspire to be would feel safe and respected.

Yet, in your daily life, it can seem, at times, that others keep handing you a script, demanding that you read the lines that someone else wrote. Family members, bosses, colleagues, even friends can direct you to move things to that conveyor belt, eat wheatgrass, drink red wine, gather prospects, sign contracts, live cruelty-free, oh, and as an afterthought "be yourself." The roar of cultural agendas, what's trending on social media, and other people's expectations of you could ride roughshod over your joy in living on this big blue planet.

To return and land solidly and consistently in who you are in your highest and best self takes self-discovery. To remain inside your experience of your truth takes strength, honesty, and vulnerability. You are so much more than a role, a title, your mistakes, your résumé, or all the times you attempted to morph according to someone else's expectations of who you should be. "Becoming You" can be the most important project you've ever been blessed to undertake, one of the most important gifts of your being alive.

May you know you are unlike anyone else on the planet.
May you see the richness of your being here and being you.

Being Seen, Heard, and Valued

"Ultimately, we all just want to be loved, heard, seen, valued, and appreciated. If each of us treated people with these core needs being met, imagine what a peaceful world this would be."
—Trina Hall

I remember going on walks with my daughter when she was a toddler. She stopped every few feet to pick up something on the ground. She examined the item with utter fascination. I had to remind myself that she really was seeing the rocks, nuts, flowers, and leaves for the first time. At preschool, she quickly learned her teachers' names, the children's names and who got along with whom. As a brilliant witness consciousness of all that happened around her, she'd come home and act out her day at school with her dolls, toys, and me. She'd freely sing the songs her classmates and teachers had sung.

The teachers thought she wasn't engaged because she often watched the other children play without engaging in the play. A keen observer, she waited patiently until she felt safe to engage. She needed to observe first and then take action. I assured the teachers that she played at home all she had absorbed at school. A foundation of structure and safety allowed my daughter to see, hear, and value what happened around her and subsequently feel seen, heard, and valued for her unique ways of being a little girl.

While I did my best to create that structure and safety in our home, my daughter and I also had our tough moments that shaped both of us. I worked diligently to break free from unhealthy patterns. I engaged rigorous healing processes that helped me see, hear, and value myself which expanded an ability to see, hear, and appreciate my daughter, later my son, and many other people in my life.

Recently, I opened up an email that asked the question "Do we value people or only reward them?" I found myself fascinated by this question, but especially the importance of valuing people whether they are family members, colleagues, friends, or employees. Do you see me? Do you hear me? Do my words mean something to your life?

Often these questions begin to be asked around age 3, when the "Look at me!" and "Look at this!" usually begins. This stage of exploration involves the development of an innate curiosity about the world around you. As an adult, you can affirm the safe explorations of small children as they make discoveries. You can connect with an awe-inspiring opportunity to see the world fresh again through the eyes of a child, which can be especially true for those of you who experienced something very different during that developmental stage.

Most young children hold no judgment about things or people. Their natural inclinations are to explore the world around them through all their senses. They're curious about everything, including the leaves, the cracks in a sidewalk, or an empty box.

The number of adults who yearn to be seen, heard, and valued makes me wonder about this need not being fully met in childhood. Sometimes this stage of development becomes difficult because connections are ruptured by adults' ignorance, their own unhealed traumas, or lack of time and presence. Some children are cruelly abused at two or three years old by adults who have not yet healed their own wounds nor learned the social, emotional, brain, and nervous system developmental needs of children. They only know to perpetuate what was done to them. These adults have not chosen to break the cycle. Hurt people hurt children. Some hurt people hurt themselves until they choose a different path.

What if your days began to fill with activities that make your heart sing, with people who actually "get you" in a deep and meaningful way? What if the most authentic and playful voices of all your inner children and adult self were heard in our world? What could or would you say? Who could you become if you knew in your heart that your curiosity and explorations of life would be celebrated by others? What could you discover about living life?

Recognizing a desire to live free and clear of past traumas or difficult experiences, to be celebrated as a multi-gifted, multi-dimensional adult can become a lifelong commitment and passion. Who you are is not limited to the functions you perform, the money you earn, the bacon you fry up in a pan, or the number of "likes" you receive on Facebook. None of these determine your value as a human being. These measures are transitory; they offer only a tiny slice at the surface of your life. You have unlimited potential and possibilities to create, explore, and transform. The quality of your life could be measured by the depth and breadth of your connections to other people, the meaningful, joyful activities that fill your days, and the positive difference your tender, soulful energy presence makes.

Being Seen, Heard, and Valued

May you look, listen, and cherish the wonderful being you have always been. May you allow yourself to be celebrated, valued, and loved. May you become full of unlimited possibilities and unleashed creativity. May many meaningful connections with others naturally emerge to nourish your one sacred life.

Love Heals

"Eventually, you will come to understand that love heals everything, and love is all there is."
—Gary Zukav

Standing at the middle of the town's main intersection for an entire year, here in Black Mountain, N.C., every Wednesday from 5 pm to 6 pm continues to be a delight. We wave, smile, and hold signs that say "Love." We've received mostly positive reactions with only a handful of not-so-positive ones. Some drivers and passengers stay completely focused on the road.

In the early weeks of our standing, I observed at different times four different men who scowled and flipped us off. One drew the gesture out fully over his head ensuring we received his complete message. Another showed us his very red, mean face as he raised his middle finger, while the female companion sitting next to him offered an enthusiastic wave with a beaming smile. This made us laugh with amazement at the stunning contrast from two people who might actually love each other. We don't know how they came to be sitting side by side in that vehicle, but a "Love" sign clearly evoked two opposite reactions.

Speaking in a phone conversation with my son about the angry finger-flippers, he simply said, "They need your love the most, Mom." What a profound truth he uttered!

At first, I felt puzzled by how anyone could scowl at a love sign until I remembered the times of fury and heartbreak when I had snarled and flipped off love.

I remembered a scene from my life years ago when I screamed "F-You!" at my first husband in front of an entire group of friends partying on a front porch on the 4th of July after he hadn't let me know where he was for the millionth time. My car tires burned rubber as I drove away in a rage declaring my own independence from his thoughtless ways, his struggles with alcohol and drugs. I had only just begun to face my own internal demons, my addiction to toxic relationships, to abusive people. Had I seen a "Love" sign that day, I might have shown my angry face while flipping up my middle finger.

Because of many skilled people who showed up with great compassion and a rich understanding of how to heal traumas, I live healthy, vibrantly alive, grateful to this day. They helped guide those wild, fierce, hot-tempered, cornered animals of past howling pain that roamed inside me to safe liberation. I began to distinguish how my wires got fired, and to cut them before those internal bombs detonated. These healers with unwavering love showed me ways that I could heal, love, and value myself from the inside out.

It's quite a challenge to offer a rope of hope when you remain tied up in your own internal knots of past unresolved heartbreaks, hurts, fears, and self-flagellations. Courageous work happens inside the back alleys of your own mind where parts of you might mug other parts of you and throw those pieces in the back of a car. Loving and valuing yourself can be the bravest work of a lifetime. Living with deeper love inside yourself, you can generously share this love fearlessly with others.

People who are hurting need your loving kindness and compassion the most. I do believe this truth in my heart of hearts. Sometimes this takes place from a distance. Occasionally you might get up close, bravely climb down into the dark hole, sit with all the pain of another human being's soul because you know what that feels like. Because you found a way to some light, fresh air, and mountain hiking trails, you become a demonstration that this is possible.

Your internal love matters. Your compassion matters. You are here to heal and love passionately, freely, as you look into your own eyes and the eyes of your fellow human beings. Love can transform your life at the heart of your hurts, in the broken open spaces of sunshine, people, traffic lights, vehicles, and poster boards bearing the red, pink, blue, purple colored word "LOVE." Love always finds a way to love. Love heals.

May you use your life energy to heal past hurts, to forgive as best you can, to emerge from that cocoon of darkness to become a bright and loving light in your time, in your unique way.

Belong to Yourself

*"Never apologize for burning too brightly or
collapsing into yourself every night.
That is how galaxies are made."*
—Tyler Kent White

My most recent hilarious "Seriously, do I have to do *this* to fit in?" moment happened when a woman I met business networking approached me at a workshop we were both attending. I did not know her well.

"Laura, when you smile, you light up a room. But your other face, and you may be concentrating, looks like you have no confidence. I recommend you hold your face like this."

She then demonstrated what looked to me like this fake bad Botox smile. I believe she was coming from a place of helpfulness, so I smiled at her.

"Thank you so much for your feedback. I really appreciate it! May I give you a hug!"

She startled, backed up a bit, but agreed to the hug. I hugged her, turned to the other woman I had been talking to and continued our conversation.

Later I wondered how long it took this woman to muster the courage to share her observation with me. I also wondered if she woke up that morning and said to herself, "Today is the day I'm telling Laura Staley what I think of her non-smiling facial expression!" Mostly, I concluded that my face triggered something for her about fitting in, about being accepted. Ultimately, her opinions about my face, smiling or not, were not about me, nor did her observations alter my commitment to belong to myself, to be myself.

I've learned that I get exhausted trying to "fit in." I've attempted in the past to become the perfect version of what I thought others wanted me to be. What I also realized is the metrics kept moving. One day I was too fat and a few years later I got accused of being anorexic. Regularly "pecked" by close others, I felt I could not ever measure up to what I now see was a certain insanity in other people's changing expectations and judgments. The person I thought I needed to become was shaped by the words, criticisms, and deeds of many other people, some of whom had a distorted view of themselves, the world, and me.

The only path that began to make sense to my soul was to become my unique self. I began to allow myself to love what I loved and to pursue my preferences, inclinations, and heart messages with a fervent passion. Often this approach involved doing the opposite of what I was told or simply exploring another pathway to my healthy, thriving life. I also observed that those who struggle to accept themselves probably won't ever accept me, no matter what I do or don't do.

Self-awareness became crucial to this journey of belonging to myself. I began to know that I am unique, that I have particular tastes, that I might learn things in a very distinct way from others around me. I began to notice that I saw the world differently than other people do, which became a gift and a challenge. I discovered I could observe all the goodness and challenges as opportunities in my day while others tended to focus on all the upsets or horrific happenings. I lived through experiences that obliterated my limiting beliefs of others or ideas I heard as a child. For instance, I was told that if you are fat and smart, no one will like you. Yet as an adult, I chose to fully embrace the body type I am, to seek knowledge from lived experiences, and create amazing bonds of lasting friendship with beloved ones who love and accept me for the person I've become.

Maybe you were told you have to be ruthless to get ahead, but then you allowed yourself to become compassionate and kind, and many opportunities to serve others began to pour into your life. You have to be willing to risk and become comfortable with the discomfort of the disapproval of others.

What path have you taken to shift from the exhausting world of "pretzeling" yourself on the altar of acceptance to embracing who you uniquely are? For some of you, like me, the path to belonging to ourselves has been hard won. You traveled on detours with a world of trolls, tortured others, well-meaning societal rule followers, and limiting-belief bearers. Others of you have been accepted by loved ones and then likely faced challenges from colleagues or bosses in a workplace or encountered societal expectations of how you should or should not behave, speak, or smile. Some of you may still be navigating this brave path or wondering why you feel so exhausted when you are with others. Fitting in can begin to fall away when you decide not to play that mental shell game because you are no longer interested.

Belonging to yourself involves being brave enough to end your cravings for the approval of others, especially those who don't know you or don't have your best interests at heart. Belonging to yourself means taking actions from your core values with full awareness that you risk being rejected by others. Yet, you recognize you won't ever desert yourself. Cultivating non-judgment for the scripts you carried around in your head that had nothing to do with being yourself brings delightful moments of relinquishing, an end to rights and wrongs, and that great divide inside of you. You begin to bring closure to your angst and to discard the imposter syndrome.

Living from your heart, inside your own skin, and your experiences of being true to yourself turns into recognizing other courageous, genuine souls who belong to themselves. You notice you can create freely, nurture compassion, and feel empathy for yourself and others. An internal sense of grace, peace, and freedom become your unshakeable companions. Your words and choices will likely annoy someone out in our world, but you will be able to go to sleep at night with a smile on your face.

May you belong fully to yourself as a self-actualized, differentiated, interdependent person, free to shine brightly.

Boundaries

Where you begin
I end.
Stay in my boat
Remain in yours.

I can only alter
My insides
Not yours.

You can only
Alter your
Outsides
Not mine.

False words
Do not match
Deeds.

Make
Amends or
Not.

Clean up
Aisle
Broken
Words or
Leave
Shattered
Glass shards.

Change behavior
As meaningful
Apology or
Not.

The story
I told
Myself
Had nothing
To do with you
And everything to do
With you.

The cleanup
In my boat

*Has everything
To do with me.*

*Your words
Deeds
Thoughts
Feelings
Are Yours.*

*My words
Deeds
Thoughts
Feelings
Are Mine.*

*No longer
A puzzle
Piece or
Object to
Be manipulated
To fit into
Your Picasso
Picture of me.*

SECTION THREE

Living Joyously

Love Aligns

Will a
Self-aware love
Wander into a
Life filled with
Heartbreak, traumas, and
Transformations?

Love attracts love.
Like attracts like.
Whole intersects whole
To find the intersection of us.

Love aligns with
Internal and external ways of
Processing the world.
In values, deep
Listening, sharing,
Humor, laughter
Six languages.

In your eyes I see myself
All the way down and inside out.

I feel your peace, dignity
Confidence, grace
Because I embrace my own.

Lovely heart butterflies land softly
On this hand
That gives away
Quiet kindness, tenderness,
With ease and
Abandon.

I didn't require a sign
From God,
Yet I receive one
With delightful surprise,
Overflowing gratitude.

In the resilience
Of this sturdy foundation,
The lightness
Of a fragile beauty
Broke free
From a puddle and a struggle
Inside a cocoon of creation.

Finding Joy in the Messes of Life

"My life has been one great big joke, a dance that's walked a song that's spoke, I laugh so hard I almost choke when I think about my life."
—Maya Angelou

A month before I signed the divorce papers, I sold the family home and moved back to the neighborhood where we had lived as a family when my children were really young. After two weeks of living in what I affectionately named, Red Cardinal House, I discovered raw sewage sludge in the basement. This stinky mess, I later learned, was caused by a hard rain, a storm-sewer backup, and a house that had been neglected for months. I felt deeply blessed that no belongings touched this black crud. I moved tub containers, luggage, a dog crate with a dog bed on top, and a beloved framed photograph my daughter took while we vacationed in Bar Harbor, Maine, into an entirely separate section of the basement.

I opened my laptop, searched for "sewage backup in basement," and called the hotline. Within an hour, a friendly man named Tommy arrived in his truck to do the cleanup. The hilarity of this latest challenge in my life bubbled up inside me as I texted friends about the crud in my basement adding that "I love my new home and I love my life. I am alive and healthy. Crud happens!" The tsunami of upheaval had not ceased. I kept surfing strong.

Tommy came to the door, saw I had a dachshund, and shared that he loves dachshunds and has two, Bacon and Brie. We bonded about our dogs. While I signed more papers, he shared the worst cleanup job he and his wife did of a home where the sewage came up to his chest. "They condemned that house. No human being could live there again." I found this disgusting, but also hilarious because he shared it with me with such passion and a smile on his face. This was a man who loves his job. I had already called my insurance company and had a claim number. I wrote out a check, which he promised to hold until the entire job was complete.

Tommy, a head taller than me with a grin and joyful aura, showed me what he'd do in the basement. His glee matched the laughter building inside of me. He began his work, and I got on the phone with my best friend. She could hardly understand me because I was laughing so hard. I snorted, cackled, and rolled on the floor with laughter. The

Universe delivered a straight-up literal message, no more metaphors. There's been some crud in my life. No kidding! And I kept cleaning up or clearing out the crud of my life … every last bit of it!

When he completed his work, Tommy did not shake my hand, but he bid me farewell and drove away. I danced on top of my bed. I flopped onto it laughing and laughing. I laughed so hard my muscles ached. I started singing really loud. No one could hear me. My son was with friends. It was Saturday night, after all. I wondered if anyone else could laugh this hard. I laughed myself to sleep.

A treasured friend sent me the text: "Sounds like you are up sh*& creek without a paddle!" which kept the laughter going the next day. I have told my closest friends to keep me humble if I ever get too full of myself, by reminding me that I had crud in my basement.

I off-loaded the woman I was and grew a new life from this fertilizer of manure. Inside all of these challenges, I found joy, freedom, a fierce spirit, a woman I didn't even recognize. In this moment, I embraced my capabilities and capacities to care for my son and daughter, two dogs (one of whom got really sick), myself, and a long list of new and old responsibilities. I cleaned, staged, sold, and packed a five-bedroom house.

With the support of treasured friends, my daughter and her friends, and the employees of Two Men and a

Truck, I moved, unpacked, and created a new home, while simultaneously nourishing my career as a feng shui consultant, and managing the fulltime work of a contested and difficult divorce. I leaned into my strength, health, and vitality, and a sense of humor through all of it. I'm forever grateful for Tommy and his passion for his work. Who knew someone could be so joyful cleaning up sh&%?

Life sends you exactly what will make you laugh because sometimes there's no other response than hysterical laughter. Laughter can keep you sane through insane experiences.

What if many things that have happened in your life could be sifted through a prism of humor? Being able to laugh comes with a healing, especially when you can laugh joyfully at yourself and the utterly ridiculous things that happen in life. A sense of humor continues to be essential alongside gratitude. Laughing and feeling grateful could easily dance together every single day.

May you see the humor giggling around some of your life experiences and laugh from deep in your belly so hard that you can no longer stand up. May you find the joy of laughing heartily at yourself because you can!

Snafus and Serendipity

"Risk-taking, trust, and serendipity are key ingredients of joy. Without risk, nothing new ever happens. Without trust, fear creeps in. Without serendipity, there are no surprises."
—Rita Golden Gelman

As I became more settled in Red Cardinal House, I noticed I lived with prison-gray walls. Several weeks after successfully navigating the sewage backup, I realized I wanted to paint the walls. I knew the gray color helped sell the house. The neutral, cool walls, the wood floors, and all the natural light flowing in through the windows inspired me. I felt welcomed by this home, which an elderly neighbor used to live in and had filled with red cardinal sun-catchers and figurines. But on an everyday basis, I experienced the gray walls quite differently.

I knew I would be having these walls painted sooner than later. I looked at my paint color fan and chose Interactive Cream, Biscuit, Totally Tan, and Ibis White. I pondered possibilities for my bedroom. Excited by the idea of an accent wall, I chose the color Free Spirit. The name made me smile.

On Monday morning I woke up singing "Climb Every Mountain" in my mind – I imagined myself as Maria Von Trapp, until discovering the poo and pee on the floor from my sweet old dog. She was blind and incontinent. I sighed and cleaned it up, with tears welling up. My love for my dogs took me to my knees with gratitude. I told myself *Breathe. This is what love does, Laura. Love cleans up the poo.* Then I fed both dogs, biked, and meditated.

With my inner world calm again, I worked at my laptop writing, editing, and building my LinkedIn profile. I paused to let out the dogs and returned to the computer on sleep mode. I hit a button; it's supposed to refresh when a key is pressed. The screen remained black. *Seriously?* I pressed another button in agitation. Blackness stared back at me. *Oh, my God, I've busted my computer. It's black-screened on me. I've lost everything!* I tried to breathe deeply. I realized that after all I had navigated this past year, inside the vortex of these types of daily snafus and much larger challenges, I held myself together with my ability to respond and redirect. *Close the computer, Laura. The Universe must need you to step away from this domain of your life.* I looked in my kitchen and saw the dark gray paint on the wall. I looked outside the window and saw the dark gray sky. *Go to the paint store! You need color in your life!* My mood shifted from anxiety to enthusiasm.

At the paint store, a tall, dark-haired young man walked over to help me. I shared my list of colors and he happily began to fill my order. He shared, "I'm going to a wedding this weekend. I'm so glad there's an open bar because that's where I'll be."

"Oh, if I were at that wedding, I'd be on the dance floor! I *love* to dance."

He then shared that he dances at a studio and if he took me as his guest, I'd get two free dance lessons.

"Really? That sounds great! I would love that!"

We exchanged information. I paid for the paint, and he carried the cans to my van. He shook my hand, assured me he'd text me, and I thanked him. Something inside me knew I would indeed be hearing from him. In the meantime, I had paint colors to test on my walls.

Free Spirit looked like pink bubblegum at nighttime on my bedroom wall, so I decided on Lavish Lavender. The gray began to disappear behind all the swatches of lovely earth tones in the other rooms. I looked forward to having the walls painted. Having some sense of accomplishment because I moved a project forward, I faced my computer's black screen with calm confidence.

All the diagnostics ran clean at the computer store. When I returned home my daughter asked me, "What button did you actually push, Mom? Show me exactly what you did, because I think you may have accidentally done a hard shutdown of your computer."

As soon as she said this, I knew that this was exactly what I had done! I started belly-laughing with relief.

"Yes! This is *exactly* what I did!"

She rolled her eyes at me, her tech-challenged mom.

On Friday evening, I began cooking a chicken stir-fry when I heard my phone ping. I noticed several texts, including one from the man at the paint store. He had invited me to the ballroom dance party. Propelled forward by excitement, I texted him that I would be there. I finished cooking that meal quickly, then put on a cute skirt and flowing cream top with black wedges. I couldn't remember the last time I felt so happy – I was going dancing! I said goodbye to my almost-adult children noting the role reversal.

I had an amazing time. The Ballroom Dance studio exuded warmth, welcome, safety, and fun. My new friend introduced me to several people and guided me through two different dances. "The Hustle" came back to me pretty quickly, and I picked up on two of the line dances fairly easily. People of all ages, body types, and skill levels stepped cautiously or flowed gracefully on the dance floor. Mostly, I felt so happy to be there surrounded by kind people and skilled instructors, who smiled and continued to invite me to dance even when I didn't know the steps. Uplifted in a way I can't even remember, I signed up for my two free dance lessons.

Sweaty and smiling, I drove back home with joy, pleasure, and enthusiasm glowing inside me, grateful for the serendipity of that trip to the paint store. Being seen through the eyes of kind strangers shifted something deep inside me. I was single, happy, and free to shine and dance! As I moved away from the gray, I discovered a more colorful world of joyous delight inside and out.

May you trust your instincts, adapt, and flow among different commitments knowing in your heart that you are being guided by love and possibilities.
May you let passion be your guide.
May you experience many delightful surprises in life.

Ladder Clatter

*"Winter, spring, summer, or fall, all you've got to do is
call and I'll be there. Yes, I will.
You've got a friend."*
—Carole King

Preparing the family house for sale, I hired a skilled, kind, and reliable handyman who introduced me to an excellent painter, who has become a forever friend. During the introduction, the handyman mentioned that we both had divorced. For me, that opened the floodgates of sharing with this gentleman. I also experienced an instant connection, like I had known him for a lifetime. As he set up his equipment, I kept talking like we had been best friends.

Some large part of me felt incredibly safe in his energy field. I trusted I could speak frankly about all I was noticing about betrayal, my anger, the fierce independent woman I was becoming, the deeper realizations that kept bubbling up about other people's choices not having anything to do with me. While on his ladder painting, he revealed that his problem was that he has a huge heart. Well, that was a lie he told himself, because his huge heart continues to be the best quality about this man, the very essence of who he is for his daughters, his friends, clients, and family.

We began texting and calling each other to connect. We showed up for each other in meaningful and empowering ways and laughed regularly at the ridiculous events that happened in our lives.

Autumn arrived and I knew I had to clear the gutters of my ranch style home. I had a ladder in the garage. Confident in my ability to use this important equipment after clearing my gutters during the past spring, I placed the ladder in the front of the house on top of grass and mulch, climbed up, and cleared away the leaves that had gathered. I felt radiant in the sunshine of the warm autumn day. As my neighbors drove by, I waved.

I then carried the ladder to the back of the house onto a cement patio with a metal bench. I placed the ladder right in back of the bench. I glimpsed the red on the bottom and stepped up several rungs when the ladder slid out from underneath me, and I fell onto the patio bruising my hip and thigh, and scraping my knees and thigh. Heart pounding and laughing with relief that the accident hadn't been more serious, I noticed that the metal bench had split in two pieces. I noted the power of gravity.

Ladder Clatter

I took a photo with my phone of the broken bench and texted a funny message to my friend. I then observed that the red I had placed on the patio had been the smooth plastic top, that the grippy red feet of the ladder had been up in the air. No wonder I fell!

My friend texted back: "Laura! I've known people who died falling off a ladder!! I'm coming over to clear your gutters. Put that ladder back in your garage! I know you are a strong, independent woman, but I want you to live!"

A couple of days later he came over, used the ladder properly, took a blower up to the roof, and blew all the rest of the leaves out of the house's gutters. When he finished, he walked me to my garage where he had hung the ladder. "Can you reach that ladder?" I said, "No. But if I got my stepladder from the kitchen, I could reach it." He began to laugh really hard. It took me a moment to realize he had intentionally hung the ladder so high that I would need assistance from a tall person to get it down. Then I laughed as I told him I had purposefully sat my Badass Self down with my Dumbass Self alongside my Wiseass Self for a three-way conversation about safety, independence, and interdependence. And I let him know, "You are the Best Guy Friend I have ever had! Thank you!"

When spring rolled around, I used the stepladder from my kitchen to get the large ladder down. With acute awareness, I placed the ladder carefully with the grippy feet always on the ground and cleared my gutters. I don't think he knows that I did that. Maybe he does. I know I can learn from my mistakes.

After too many years of having my competence and intelligence questioned, demeaned, or belittled by my ex and other individuals who held poisonous righteousness about their way or the highway, I became a fierce warrior for my intelligence, capacities, ways of thinking and doing things. I continue to stand for my truth, the experiences I've lived. I'm incredibly grateful this ladder lesson got delivered in a relatively soft way. This incident remains a reminder that I will continue to make mistakes, that I can ask for support from quality, trustworthy people, and that I have great friends who show up for me.

Cultivating an ability to laugh at yourself and your mistakes can be such a liberation. Knowing when to ask for support from an empowered place rather than helplessness lives like a wonderful shift. No longer a victim, you can collaborate and work with others in meaningful, life-enriching ways. You are able and capable. You are stronger than your small mind thinks.

Ladder Clatter

May you know your strengths and see your humanity with humor. May you know the rich experience of great friends who support and laugh with you.

Gratitude as a Catalyst

"Gratitude opens the door to ... the power, the wisdom, the creativity of the universe. You open the door through gratitude."
—Deepak Chopra

I almost lost my son to death twice. Then a day arrived that I got a voicemail message from the house where my son resided. I learned that he had walked out of the house with no phone, no money, just the shoes on his feet and the clothes on his body in LA. The staff member shared about the stresses my son had been navigating. Staff members were out on the streets searching for him. They promised to call me. I wept when I got off the phone. My heart raced with panic as my mind filled with images of my son wandering the streets amidst other homeless people or dead in a ditch. I interrupted this by calling all my closest friends to request their support, prayers, love, care, however they wanted to send good energy to my son and me. My day of writing and editing came to an abrupt, heart-wrenching halt.

I drove to a church. I hadn't walked into a church in years. I made my way to what I discovered later was the Children's Chapel. Sitting down in a pew in the silence and beauty of the stained-glass windows, I wept. I moved to the front of the chapel where two chairs faced each other. I removed my clogs, lay down with my legs over one of the chairs in my favorite meditation pose, and closed my eyes. Scenes of my son's life downloaded in a flowing stream – all the things he loved, including his passion for Star Wars, Legos, and running. I kept placing all in God's hands because there was absolutely nothing tangible I could do to save my son's life this time. I began shaking from the delayed shock response, a familiar sensation in my body. I gathered my belongings, my tiny bit more centered soul and called a dear friend.

"I need to say this out loud because it helps me to know I have a plan. He really may be found dead, and I need to know that I can call you and come to your home if that happens to be the reality." I choked out these words. I knew having a plan would provide some safety and structure in the midst of a heart implode.

"I am here for you. I have you, Laura. I love you. Your son is so smart, Laura; he'll find his way back to the house."

Gratitude as a Catalyst

I appreciated her confidence in my son. Another friend called as I pulled in my driveway. She asked if she could pray out loud for both my son and me. Her voice, love, passion, faith flowed into my being like a cascading warm waterfall of grace. I wept. She asked what I was doing next. I promised I would eat because I hadn't eaten a thing for hours.

My mind continued to play out his death as I thought about how people often arrive with food when someone dies. People hold you, hug you, wrap their arms around you, feed you. None of this happened during these hours of tortured waiting because I refused to disrupt other people's lives; I had learned long ago how to survive being alone during s*&^ storms.

Another friend called and we discussed all the different scenarios. Speaking them out loud calmed me for a moment. She encouraged me to write everything I felt and experienced.

I gathered some of my son's most beloved childhood belongings at the table where I wrote. I sat down, opened my laptop, and typed "My Precious Boy My Precious Son: Living with Uncertainty, Letting Go and Letting God." And my phone rang.

"Hello, this is Laura."

"Laura, your son is at the house. He is safe and telling us he is sober. He's telling another staff member he had an epiphany. He's been up all night and did not sleep. He recognized he was homeless. He saw a lot of homeless people. We will be having many conversations with him. He will have consequences. I will have him call you in about an hour."

I barely choked out my words I was crying so hard.

"Thank you so much. Thank you. Thank you. Thank you. I am so relieved. Thank you. Thank God."

I kept typing. The phone rang. "Hi, Mom."

"I love you so much. I will always love you no matter what. I'm so grateful you are safe, sober, and back at the house. I love you. I love you."

He explained that he finally chose sobriety 100 percent for himself. Sobriety wasn't being forced on him. He chose his life with every cell of his being.

I know in my bones how sacred and precious life is. Grateful is not a big enough word for what I experience when I hear his voice full of presence and vitality on the phone each time he's called since that day. Though I no longer get to look in his eyes or hug him and tell him, "I love you!" daily, our heart connection remains strong, clear, and deep. For those who have lost a child, I recognize I only placed a big toe and pulled it back out from an ocean of "grieflove" you swim in every day.

Practicing gratitude consistently for several years now, I notice that I'm reaping the benefits of an internal world

Gratitude as a Catalyst

filled with more moments of peace, profound grace, and briefer periods of grief. I continue to cry easily for all the good in my life, for this deep sense of safety I now live with, for the love and appreciation that spill over in my interactions with many others. Shifting my focus to gratitude for the sake of the heart-opening, brain-rewiring benefits began an enduring transformation in the quality of my life. No matter what has gone before me or what will happen tomorrow, I feel grateful.

When you have endured loss, you actually can experience gratitude from a heightened awareness and a place that endures over time. You can hold both experiences in your heart of the ache and the fresh, full new day that calls to you. Grieving is a kind of gratitude because it means you continue to love deeply. You are thankful for the broken-open heart that unleashes gushy tenderness, affection, and appreciation out into our world.

Knowing that you may choose to hold your loved ones in your arms with much tenderness this evening, that you can appreciate the simple meal on your dinner table, that the next breath you take can be a deep one from your diaphragm, that your kind words and genuine smile for a stranger can be generously given, all demonstrate the power of thankfulness to imbue your life with an energy that opens doors and windows to that which remains a wellspring of inspiration.

Where there once were only walls, may a practice of gratitude gently turn the doorknobs of the doors of your life and allow you to walk out into the bright sunshine of this day, this most glorious day.

Flight Wings of Kindness

"Hello, sun in my face. Hello, you who made the morning and spread it over the fields...Watch, now, how I start the day in happiness, in kindness."
—Mary Oliver

Leaving to visit my son for the first time since he left Columbus, I boarded a plane for a flight to Los Angeles with a stop in Las Vegas. I took the middle seat next to a man sitting by the window, and a young college-aged woman took the aisle seat. I looked up and noticed in the aisle a man and woman who seemed distressed.

"I really must sit with my wife." He looked concerned and glanced around at the seated passengers, who made no eye contact with him. He repeated this request two more times. The woman sitting next to me unbuckled, got up, and moved to a seat in the back of the plane. Like a synchronized swimmer, I immediately followed suit, quickly finding an aisle seat on the other side, a row behind this couple. All three of us settled into our seats.

The man looked back at me with utter relief.

"Thank you so much, Miss."

The fact that he addressed me as "Miss" filled my heart with such joy that I hardly processed his gratitude, because it had been years since anyone had referred to me as "Miss." Relocating was easy; I was traveling alone.

During the four-hour flight, I glanced over several times. I noticed that the man kept his arm around his wife the entire flight. They cuddled while watching a movie on a phone he held in his right hand. My heart filled with warmth as I witnessed this loving interaction. I felt happy that the young woman and I moved so they could have this experience.

Once off the plane in Las Vegas, I made a beeline for the terminal where the gate for the flight to Los Angeles was located. Focused and intentional, I hardly noticed anything except the signs guiding me to Terminal C. Arriving with plenty of time to spare, I spotted a juice bar with no line. I placed an order and heard a man's voice behind me.

"May we please pay for your drink, Miss?"

I turned around to see the couple from the first leg of the flight glowing at me. Tears welled in my eyes as I struggled for a moment to speak.

"That is so sweet and yes, you may. That is so kind of you!"

"We want to thank you so much for giving up your seat so we could sit together. We recently got married, and this was our first plane ride together."

"Oh, congratulations! That's so wonderful!"

We hugged one another and chatted some more. We exchanged business cards. When the man looked at my card, he said to his wife, "She's a feng shui consultant!"

He knew how I helped people! My fruit smoothie showed up on the counter. I thanked them again, picked up my beverage, and walked to the black-vinyl and stainless-steel chairs at the gate. I was so moved I almost cried. I thought about how he called me "Miss" twice, and it thrilled me. I also had two revelations about my life in relation to the many kind strangers I have encountered: *I love people, and I'm never alone in the world!*

I remembered Wayne Dyer talking about looking for opportunities every day to help someone, a practice he offered as a way to begin to reach beyond the ordinary and into the extraordinariness of life. Thinking about the everyday subtle flow of generous giving and gracious receiving happening between many people in the small moments of human interaction heartened me.

Scientists know that giving, receiving, or even witnessing an act of kindness strengthens the immune system and increases serotonin, a neurotransmitter that regulates mood in the brain. This remains great news for humanity. Kind actions create a ripple effect, as people feel better after such interactions and then choose to pay kind deeds forward. In this larger context, acts of kindness can be a path to wellness for the larger community. You don't need to wait for natural disasters or human tragedies to connect with others with presence, kindness, and awareness. There's positive energy and majesty in gentleness and simple acts of human compassion, and everyone benefits.

May kindness be what you practice first towards yourself and extend to many others from a deep well of love.

Allow Joy to Lift You

"Have only love in your heart for others. The more you see the good in them, the more you will establish good in yourself."
—Paramahansa Yogananda

To hear the pure joy and clarity in my son's voice when he calls me from LA is like no other experience. One afternoon he called to share with me that he really got what I'd been talking about throughout his childhood.

"Mom, I noticed a man needed help carrying his tray at McDonald's, so I lifted the tray to his table. Then he asked me if I'd unwrap his sandwich. I did so. The man thanked me. As I turned to walk away, I glanced back and saw he had no hands…he was bent over, eating his sandwich, Mom!"

My son's voice choked.

"Mom, I have hands! I am here, alive! I can be of love and service to many others! I really see that I'm a spiritual being having a human experience!"

Tears welled in my eyes as my throat squeezed and a warm internal tingling shower flowed throughout my body.

"I love you so much. Indeed, you are an amazing soul on the planet. I'm proud of you. I love you so much. I'm grateful you see this. May you know this forever in your heart."

He and I had lived through many joyous, connected, then painful, heartbreaking, and hellishly terrifying experiences together. His unfolding story of transformation continues to be one that brings many tears of gratitude. As his mom, I hold his goodness, his wholeness, and the essential nature of his personality. Stories of the joy and fears of intuitively knowing a baby boy grew in my womb, and experiencing his birth, his life as a baby, toddler, little boy, and young teenager have embedded themselves in my soul. His gifted and talented intellect match his empathy, sensitive nature, and compassion. And yet, despite his gifts, he took himself to dark places that I could not fathom. I loved him no matter what.

During a deeper reflection, you realize moments of great joy in your life often involve other human beings, loving interactions, those experiences of seeing the beauty and goodness in another. Have you been listening for the treasures in other people in your life? Sometimes these people don't fully embrace their multifaceted capacities, so

Allow Joy to Lift You

you can become the gift seer, the guide to the goodness they sometimes struggle to see in themselves.

Do you have the capacity to see and hold people's light even when they've shrouded themselves in darkness, denial, and disgust? Even when they have uttered pain-filled words and committed thoughtless deeds? Are there people in your life who believe in you on your worst days, during the dark nights of your life?

Every single person on your life path who sees your light, who has forgiven your mistakes and miscues and still believes that you matter, deserves your profound gratitude. These people who hold you high, even when you can barely pull yourself out of the latest muddy ditch, deserve your appreciation.

You may, at times, struggle to see yourself through their eyes, and yet, despite your struggle, they keep beaming love and luminous light your way. Their warm hands reach out to hold yours; their arms pull you in for a big hug. These precious individuals may have lived in the background of your life as you grew up. You may barely know they cheer for you even today, but they model what you can do for yourself. Observing their example, you can see ways to generously give to others.

The benefits of emptying out the detritus inside your heart allow you to be fully present with the wholeness of others, their unspoken hurts, spoken joys, and undistinguished or minimized gifts. With softer eyes and a heart full of compassion, you can begin to see beauty everywhere in people you meet. Your expanding capacity for paying attention to the astonishing multiple talents in those you encounter opens the door to appreciation and an ability to remain dedicated to their meaningful lives. You want others to thrive. You want them to wake up filled with a deeper appreciation of the life they get to live.

May you use your life energy every day going forward to honor these beloved individuals by creating a life you love living, in gratitude, in honor of those who remain genuine treasures in your life. May you extend this grace, compassion, and joy in being alive to the next person you meet. May you give the unexpected gift of kindness from your beautiful, humble heart.

He Had Me at Mary Oliver

*"Believe in love. Believe in magic. Believe in others.
Believe in yourself. Believe in your dreams.
If you don't, who will?"*
—Jon Bon Jovi

During the time period after my life rapidly altered from being married with two children, two dogs, and a husband to being single with one dog, I chose to courageously leap into the world of online dating. With encouragement from a friend, I signed up on a site. I really needed a Sherpa guide as I had no idea what I was doing. I began answering all the different questions. In response to "Who are you looking for?" I wrote, "Someone who will make me laugh." That's it. I pondered the question, "What is your username?" I thought about how much I loved the poetry of Mary Oliver, that my favorite poem was "Wild Geese." I figured the dudes out in internet land would know that "MO" are the initials for Mary Oliver, that they would be familiar with her beautiful poetry. I created my username: WildGeeseMO11.

After initially freaking out over the "blow up" of email messages that arrived, I got brave and opened one. Thinking to myself this guy was born in 1969, I clicked PassionPlay69. He shared about liking the Buckeyes, dark chocolate, walking in the woods. He let me know he was a social drinker and asked if I liked s'mores. I replied. "I like the Buckeyes, chocolate, and walking in the woods. I don't drink but I have plenty of friends who enjoy a glass of wine. No problem with the social drinking. I'm gluten-free so I can't do the graham crackers, but I like toasted marshmallows and chocolate. Haven't had a s'more in years."

That morning on my run I kept wondering about "PassionPlay69" and then the translation hit me. OMG!! I did the Eeew dance and met with one of my closest women friends later that day. I told her everything.

"You are not going walking in the woods with this guy. No! You never put 'wild' in anything on the internet with dudes and dating! And we must look up s'mores in Urban Dictionary! You must shut down your profile on that site! Today!"

"What's Urban Dictionary?" I quietly asked. I had no clue.

"A dictionary for slang used on the internet. Oh, here's what s'mores means! OMG!"

I closed down the site. I chose to go the old-fashioned pathway to meet a kind, self-aware man in person. I removed the framed art piece in my bedroom of a single woman with her back to me. I created and hung a collage of images of couples laughing, holding hands, kissing in natural settings. I purchased *21 Days to the Love of Your Life* by Kac Young. Journaling answers to the 36 questions for 45 minutes every single day for 21 days, I cried as I poured out of my heart all I had dreamed about since my teen years. "Self-aware" showed up all over the pages. On day 22, I burned all of that ink and paper on a cold, starry February night out on my patio a few days after Valentine's Day. Befriending two really great, smart, kind men opened my heart, bolstered my confidence, and assured me I had the capacity to care, connect, laugh, cry, and heal. Both men remain treasured people in my life. Our friendships endure.

One year and 7 months after I closed down the internet dating site and two months after burning the journal on my patio, I attended a Singles Mingle Meetup at a restaurant where eight men and four women gathered. Having done a great deal of business networking, I chose to see this experience in a similar light. I introduced myself to two men and a woman. I listened as they shared about travel, art museums, and their favorite national parks. I shared about being an author, showed them my book, and let them know how much I loved nature, being outside, experiencing beautiful artwork. I gave the two men my business card as I got ready to leave as I had another commitment. I noticed the one gentleman literally twinkled at me when he smiled. He sent an email that evening asking if I would like to meet for coffee.

I replied, "Yes, but I don't usually drink coffee." He responded, "That's okay. I don't drink coffee." This became one small "in common" of a thousand. We met and hit it off quite beautifully. I really enjoyed his company, our conversation. We walked outside at parks and through neighborhoods after getting a beverage. On our third date while sitting across from each other in a Panera there was an unusual lull in the conversation. I asked him.

"Do you enjoy reading?"

"Well, yes, lately I've been reading the poetry of Mary Oliver before I go to sleep at night."

"Yaaaaaaah!!!!" I screamed with delight while waving my arms in the air.

I told him the entire internet debacle story. He laughed, then asked how he could be of service. I told him the truth about wanting to be in a love relationship. He said he wasn't looking. I shared that we could be friends, that I could date a bunch of men. The playful interacting and laughing continued as he walked me to my minivan. He asked to purchase a copy of my book. I handed him a book.

He then looked at me and said, "You know. I'm open to love." He gently kissed me before we parted ways.

What my heart had desired for a lifetime happened. Relinquishing a strong attachment to a result freed me. I became open, more loving, happier, and more liberated than before I walked into that restaurant on that glorious spring day. I felt love on the inside that endures to this day. A holistic transformation gradually took place. Taking brave actions became easier as I noticed how much better I felt. Giving myself permission to feel good reminded me of how I often share this gold nugget with my *Cherish Your World* clients.

To live a fulfilling life, you must take risks for your dreams. Whatever your deep desire, taking many micromovements alongside big leaps of faith can land you in that whole new world inside your heart and out in your life. Fear begins to slide into the background as love and passion grow. The idea that there's one secret, one action, or overnight results does not match most backstories of diligent, small daily steps people take to build a life they love living. Sometimes shifting requires releasing limiting beliefs, engaging new practices, letting go of all types of clutter, and opening yourself to brand new experiences.

Softening the hands and the heart is well worth the experience of laughing much and often.

May you find and create healthy bonds with beloved ones who see your goodness and gifts and you see theirs. May you find common ground with high-quality people. May you hold one another high.

Hang On–Help Is On Its Way

"When you trust in yourself, you are trusting in the same wisdom that created you."
—Wayne W. Dyer

Getting in my vehicle after writing with a friend at the library, I put my key in the ignition and turned it, and all I heard was a click. I laughed because my friend just handed me a book titled *The Universe Has Your Back: Transform Fear to Faith* by Gabrielle Bernstein. In this moment, I felt relaxed despite my minivan's dead battery. It's the third recent mishap involving my vehicle, and things seemed to happen in threes. My friend offered to get me my favorite drink from a local coffee shop. I found my AAA membership card and called for emergency road service.

Cloudy, windy, and chilly on this autumn day, I stood next to my vehicle feeling peaceful and looking for the AAA truck. My friend returned. I thanked and hugged her, so grateful for the warm drink. She drove away confident in my capacities. I had been living single for over two years and this situation seemed entirely manageable.

The AAA truck pulled up and the driver got out. He was a handsome young man wearing an army ball cap and the AAA fluorescent yellow jacket. We began a conversation as he checked the battery. I quickly learned that he serves in the Army Reserves and he is engaged.

"I hope I'm not being too personal, but how did you propose to your fiancée?"

I was genuinely interested. He was being so open and chatty that I figured, why not? He then told a story of sharing his decision with his parents, asking her parents for their blessing, collaborating with his mom on the purchase of the ring, getting the ring, being awake for 24 hours in different airports, making his way back to his girlfriend in Columbus, and finally "taking a knee on the 20-yard line" in the Columbus airport in front of his girlfriend, circled by family members who cheered and cried. She said yes with tears of joy and surprise. He showed me the photo of the moment on his phone.

I felt thrilled to be meeting a man who relishes the telling of the proposal story as much as many women do. It's heartening to know men like this exist! (It's not that I didn't think they did; it's that I hadn't had personal experience with them.) I asked him his name and he shared his first name. I felt a motherly bond with this young man.

"That's my son's name!"

During this conversation, I got a call from a friend, who offered to bring me lunch because she happened to be in the neighborhood and wanted to see me. She arrived with sweet potato fries and veggie burgers. While the young man installed the new battery and processed the paperwork, my friend and I hungrily ate our fries in her warm car, and I shared the happy experiences I was having during this battery breakdown. As I noticed the man finishing up, I climbed out of her car and shook hands with him. He seemed like a person my son might be in five years.

"Be certain to keep looking for new ways to love your fiancée! She's so fortunate to have you in her life!"

"Oh, I will! I'm cooking dinner for her tonight. She cooked chicken Alfredo last night, and I will cook her a delicious dinner tonight!"

He climbed into the AAA truck and drove away. I stood in the chilly wind, warmed by joy and inspiration. That's what love does: Love keeps looking for new ways to express itself as kind deeds, appreciation, inspiring stories from a stranger who started to feel like a family member, and a new battery full of life and energy to drive my vehicle into a future of more possibilities and loving experiences.

I believe a higher power showed up as a kind, talkative man who, in addition to installing a new battery, shared his light of service and joy in being alive and in love. Faith showed up as beloved friends bringing a hot beverage and a meal. I imagine that reading Gabrielle's book will be validation and reinforcement for the strategy of being ready for whatever comes my way, comfortable leaning into others and knowing it will be all right.

Maybe the Universe or a higher power always has your back, and perhaps your higher power is assisted by loved ones – the sort of people who show up to hand you tea and sweet potato fries on a chilly autumn day.

May you be the inspired being naturally willing to share your love and light with a stranger, a customer, or a friend. May you be a person willing to receive the kindness of loved ones, the enthusiasm and joy of many helpful people on your travels.

Create Space for Joy

"A dream that will need all the love you can give, every day of your life, for as long as you live. Climb every mountain…"

—Richard Rogers and Oscar Hammerstein

On a bitterly cold day in Ohio, my Sweet Love and I began a conversation about spending the winter in a warmer climate. We became very inspired by the possibility of relocating. The research began in earnest for a new place to live that would have more days of sunshine, warmer temperatures, culture, and nature.

One day he texted me, "If you could live anywhere, where would you like to live?

Without hesitation, I texted back, "Asheville, NC."

The next day he texted me: "We can move there. Would you like to move there?"

I thought we were brainstorming, still researching possibilities. My heart pounded. During an in-person conversation that evening, he assured me that he meant what he had messaged me.

From deep inside of my gut and soul, I said, "Yes!" We hugged, high-fived, danced, and cheered.

I had fallen in love with the Blue Ridge Mountains years ago. I also realized that on the walls of every place I had lived, including my college dorm rooms, I had placed posters or framed photographs of mountains, a feng shui environmental affirmation long before I knew about this ancient wisdom. Additionally, *The Sound of Music* remains my favorite musical ever. Maria Von Trapp, portrayed by Julie Andrews, who I also love to this day, became a joyous role model for me at six years old. I wanted to emulate her in every single way that I possibly could, especially the opening scenes of her singing and dancing in the mountains. I watch this movie at least once a year, if not more.

Once again, the Universe or Someone seemed to have my back because without doing any research on whether my house in Ohio would even sell or thinking about the thousand things that could've had me reconsider, we happily took actions that happened easily, almost effortlessly, and in a relatively short time period.

He had never been to Asheville, so I wanted to be certain he would love it. We scheduled a trip to investigate. He loved the area. Driving to many different communities, we easily narrowed down the town in which we wanted to live. I met with my favorite realtor, who assured me it was a great time to sell in my neighborhood. I hired my amazing, cherished contractors, who had done excellent work for me previously to make additional improvements in the house. I dug up hundreds of dandelions in the front yard. My Sweet Love and I sold our vehicles. I purchased a Subaru to handle the mountain roads. He got a Jeep. I let go of even more belongings once we found our places to live in Black Mountain.

The whirlwind of activity brought me such joy. Even knowing I would be leaving the most loving friends and colleagues I have ever known, which made me tear up regularly, I also felt a liberation in my being that I had not ever experienced in my lifetime. Knowing I'd be leaving my daughter also squeezed my heart, made me weep. Yet I trusted, still trust, the strong bond we continue to cultivate. Plus, she could teach me how to FaceTime.

I kept telling people that I felt like a young person finally going away to college! The idea of not seeing all the familiar reminders of the spaces and places that tethered me to the person I no longer was thrilled me. The inner feng shui coming home to my soul created a life-changing outer transformation that I could not have predicted.

There are those of you feeling obligated to do activities that make your stomach hurt. Distinct from the butterflies in the tummy of excitement or some anxiety from stretching into the zone of uncomfortable for a big cause, I'm talking about the dread and resentment that makes you feel exhausted before you start. Can you set these activities free from your life now and possibly forever? These "to do's" most likely remain out of alignment with your reason for being here on the planet. Can you place them on the "Chuck It" list?

What's going on in your life that demands your full attention? What can you bravely walk away from? Disconnecting from activities or relationships or a place that no longer serve your life can be profound and liberating. You may get blowback from people who feel threatened by your choices, whatever these may be. You may risk rejection; yet, you will be able to live with yourself. You might sleep more deeply at night knowing you finally at this pivotal moment listened to your soul's calling, your heart's whisperings.

Create Space for Joy

*May you set free what suffocates you. May you use your life energy to do what you love. May you shred the outdated script someone handed you decades ago. May you find the courage to design a life you love living. May you make room for healing that creates space for joy. Life is now.
May you live it fully.*

Live Like It Matters

"The most beautiful people we have known are those who have known defeat, known suffering, known struggle, known loss, and have found their way out of the depths. These persons have an appreciation, a sensitivity and an understanding of life that fills them with compassion, gentleness, and a deep loving concern. Beautiful people do not just happen."
— Elisabeth Kübler-Ross

While living in North Carolina continues to free me, I still grieve as I miss my beloved ones I no longer see on a weekly or daily basis. Nothing replaces in-person time with people with whom I have created strong bonds of love and care. I miss my adult children. I live in this messy middle place of incredible freedom of expression in my writing, daily activities, new experiences, and missing people who enrich my life beyond measure.

As someone who has constantly yearned for the "happy ending" where finally the characters have all that they've ever dreamed about, I realize that each choice I make comes with a mixture of utter gratitude and missing the large container of honey that didn't make it on the moving van, my bike rides along the Olentangy River, and the people I love.

Bravely letting go of some of the rich experiences I enjoyed from my old life continues to be important grownup work. My choice to move to the mountains altered those experiences, the structures I had created. Touch and quality time are my top two languages of love as I notice myself regularly petting my dog, Layla, and hugging my Sweet Love as much as I can. If I could look into the eyes of all my beloved ones, including my two adult children right now and say to their beautiful faces, "I love you!" and hug them, I would do that in a heartbeat.

I've learned to savor, to be fully present for what seem like fleeting moments with people I cherish when I return to Columbus or they visit me here in N.C. I know the high value of love, of connection in my life. I also fiercely value my liberation from all that kept me small and contained. I sometimes vacillate between loving my freer, quieter existence on the side of a mountain and yearning for what I left behind in central Ohio. And there's no turning backwards, for I have found my voice, the seat of my soul, and a home for my heart. I'm clear I made a healthy leap into a new life.

Letting go courageously sometimes involves releasing what you love, have loved, will always love. You bravely say goodbye to your lovable dying pet, your dear friend as cancer wins, a career you appreciated for decades. You may have lost a beloved spouse who savored life up to her last breath. Sometimes life crashes over you with the loss of several people you love in rapid succession.

Losses can take you to your knees or your bed with unrelenting grief. On the other hand, the ocean wave of goodbyes can also spark you to live every day with fierce, unstoppable passion, gratitude, tenacity, and resilience. You realize death and loss each painfully teach you how to live like everything matters.

In your physical spaces, many of you realize you must part ways with belongings you still love because of downsizing to a much smaller living space, making a conscious choice to simplify, or finally beginning to make peace with a dream that won't ever be fulfilled.

Sometimes there's no preparation for the brave relinquishing of a beloved one, a belonging, or your usual routine. If you've ever had something stolen, experienced a fire or flood, suffered the unexpected death of a loved one, or an injury or a health challenge, you know what I'm describing.

With heartbreak and complete surrender to uncertainty, to the unknown in the next moment, you say goodbye to who and what embodied love and support. This departure may create an existential challenge in your entire being. In that place of disorientation, you realize how much you've cultivated a huge capacity to love. Eventually there may be a time for radical acceptance or maybe that experience remains elusive. In the meantime, grieving continues to be a process that will have its own way with your very essence.

Sometimes there's a peeling away until you find yourself at the very center of what you deeply value about being alive, what matters most to you. The journey inside you becomes urgent and necessary for your ability to rise with resilience, to transcend, to live free. Fully facing the impermanence of all that lives outside of you, you can begin to flourish as an awakened being, an untethered soul.

No one was ever yours to have forever. No belonging was ever yours to hold forever. Love never left you forsaken because love lives strong inside of you and always will as life flows through you.

May you live in the flow of each day with your heart always open. May you graciously let go and receive with soft hands all that leaves and comes. May you no longer hold back what you have to offer. My you live like every moment matters.

Magical Mountain

I see Mama
And Baby Bear
Peeking at me
Through
Bushes
Amidst
The trees.

Awake, aware,
In awe
We stare.

Your sweet
Faces etched
In my internal
Flash drive.

You remind
Me how
Delightful it
Is to be alive.

I hear
Branches breaking
Ahead of us.
Papa emerges
Large and lumbering.
I wonder
If you'll find
Those bees
Humming.

Tailgating
In the back
Of the Jeep
Mama and Baby
Snack.

It's football
Season
Time to live
Off the beaten
Track.

Now peering in
Our porch window

*I'm in the
Zoo.
For we are
In your woods
Of glorious leaves
And glistening dew.*

*Baby bear
Romps solo,
Poses,
Climbs steps.
I smile,
Breathe,
Click photos.
Look for
Mama.
Nowhere in
Sight…yet!*

*Not in
Kansas anymore
With my little
Dog, too.
Childlike*

Joy envelops
And holds
With glitter glue.

Gleeful and Giddy
Like
Grown Up Goldilocks
Living in a
House of Joy
On this magical mountain
With her
Sexy Silver Fox.

SECTION FOUR

Living Beyond

Soar

Somewhere beyond
Fitting inside
Cramped spaces,
Suffocating,
Shape shifting,
Societal mores,
Outdated expectations,
A rogue heart beats
Hungry.

Something sits beside
the dull blade of fear,
Beneath the surface of
Noisy promises,
Above hurt,
Inside
Imagination.

Unrecognizable music
Awakens what
Died long ago.

Burst free from
The cage of bones.

Live in the billowing
Mist, the lake
Reflections,
Millions of colorful
Leaves fluttering,
Dancing in the
Bright blue
Stratosphere of
Sacred
Light, in this
Moment
Lifted,
Fed by
Eternity.

A Fresh Start

"New beginnings are often disguised as painful endings."
—Lao Tzu

A close friend tearfully shared with me the story of one of her good friends leaving for California. A few days after her farewell party, the friend, who had just gone through a painful divorce, boarded a plane carrying only personal items and left behind most of her belongings in a rental home. She had never departed like this before. None of her closest friends knew the condition of the house she left.

Twelve shocked women descended on the home she left and within two days cleared the perilously cluttered basement and all other rooms of the house to make space for a new renter. Her friends gave unselfishly of their time and elbow grease, realizing their friend, now in California, may have felt embarrassed about the condition of her life and her home. She needed formidable vulnerability and courage to admit to the pain and clutter of her life, even to her closest friends.

My friend then shared that the situation felt like a wakeup call for her. She confessed she tends not to tell people about the hard things going on in her life or ask others for help when she's struggling. I don't think she's alone in this desire to hide and hold it all together rather than risk exposure.

I remember quickly packing the cluttered, disorganized kitchen of a friend who was moving at the same time she was bravely battling cancer. Another friend and I looked at each other when we saw the state of her kitchen. "I guess our friend is a bit of a hoarder." I nodded. We rolled up our sleeves and threw away a varied assortment of science experiments from her fridge. We opened drawers and placed items in boxes as efficiently as possible. We loved our friend and knew she was doing the best she could.

The woman who flew to California may have had relatives who did not approve of her move. It seems she wanted freedom from her past, *all* of her past, so she left it behind. Having invested time and love in vibrant friendships, she trusted that these women would be there for her in a time of need, even though she hadn't disclosed her troubles. She accepted that compassionate friends will do what needs to be done for a beloved one.

A Fresh Start

Have you ever walked away or wanted to walk away from your entire life and start fresh? What do you do when you need to let go and bravely start over? Do you reach out for support when life gets challenging?

Sometimes, for a variety of reasons, you may choose to stop, drop, and get on a plane. In certain situations, this desire to be free may be so strong that it outweighs the consequences of real or perceived shame, failures, challenges, and hidden clutter in your home. Yearning for a fresh start can drive your actions. You may even be willing to risk your reputation as a "got it all together" person.

You may not want others to know your challenges and how cluttered your basement really is. You may fear you look like a hoarder to your friends, and some part of you knows there is an interdependent relationship with our lives, homes, and psyches. Maybe you haven't invited friends over to your home for months because of this embarrassment or admitted to yourself what is painful in your life. You might think you are alone, so consequently, you exhaust yourself by striving to appear that you have it all together, to fit in, and to seem "normal."

What if you realized that most people have some or a lot of clutter that matches a handful or many challenges in their lives? Knowing this, could you then breathe, relax, and reach out for some support? Many people have faced a home or life challenge at some point. You are not alone. You deserve a fresh start. You need courage to slowly dissipate the perfectionist pretense, but your heart can be grateful for those who care about you and most likely will want to help.

Reaching out to others for support in times of challenge might be part of a new beginning. There's a shared humanity that happens in times of transition. You often see that you are perfectly imperfect and utterly human.

The invitation exists for you to be courageously vulnerable in your life and, through that moment, you may realize that honest communication with others makes the challenges a bit more bearable. Uncomfortable, vulnerable conversations can result in more meaningful bonds and a realization that you are connected in love and compassion with caring people.

A fresh start often involves gently letting go of shame, embarrassment, mistakes, failures, doubt, and limiting beliefs. New beginnings include embracing our deep desire for freedom, growth, and fulfilling, honest relationships with others. Clutter doesn't define you; you can clear it away along with disempowering thoughts that can dissipate over time. The rewards of a new moment, a clean canvas, and a more vibrant home are worth the effort.

A Fresh Start

May you find the courage to drop the pretense of perfection and discover a wealth of support from compassionate, loving people. May you create fresh beginnings every day of your life as you bravely shed the remnants of the past that no longer uplift you.

A Beautiful Interior by Design

"We can never make peace in the outer world until we make peace in our inner world."
—*The Dalai Lama*

As I compose this essay, my wallet remains missing. The place I'm fairly certain I left it had a note on the door "Back by 3 pm." I made phone calls, sent texts, and will return to The Cutting Crew this afternoon here in Black Mountain. I imagine a relieved reunion with my blue wallet. I'm choosing to trust, an unusual liberating response. Past experiences have finally taught me that the unknown or the uncertain do not have to be scary. Lessons in the rewards of paying attention alongside compassion for my imperfect humanity continue to keep me grounded in humility.

As I look out at the lush green trees, the bright fuchsia blossoms on the rhododendron bush, the asparagus sprouts, roses, irises, and overgrown wild bushes, I feel peaceful.

This new neighborhood remains exquisitely gorgeous everywhere my eyes can see. The quiet at night, the birds chirping in the morning, the ripples on the lake where I run, the sound of the geese, the sight of the ducklings and goslings, the gravel path with green sensuous mountains all around nourish my inner life.

I just got a call from Joe, the owner of the hair salon. He has my blue wallet. It turns out that he drove to the house last night to drop it off, but I was at the lake on an evening walk. A tearful, happy, grateful reunion with my wallet can now happen. A gentler inner world dances with a life filled with kind, generous people. I observe consistent creative bursts, a greater ability to respond calmly, and a childlike spontaneity that would make both of my adult children happy.

Your interior world may be enriched by other types of sensory experiences. Maybe you prefer a coffee shop with music, lights, and people gathered, or an urban setting with bustle and brilliance. Notice there's a dynamic relationship happening between outer spaces and your inner world of body sensations, thoughts, emotions, breath, and quiet. No matter where you are, you take your inner world with you.

Have you taken time to enhance your internal house with lightness and blissful decor? Is it time to claim your unique way of arranging the furniture of your focus, values, and passion? Have you begun to cultivate a witness who

A Beautiful Interior by Design

watches peacefully without judgment from a comfy chair or a padded seat of your soul? Could you finally take down the creepy artwork of your nightmares? Are you willing to dismantle the shields and thick walls of anger you've placed around your hurting heart? Are there dressers and cabinets in your mind filled with loving memories you've forgotten?

I recognize we live in a culture that tends to be outward focused on the bling, pings, and pitches. Sometimes easily distracted by what's going on in the world of people, belongings, interactions, and the ever-changing everything, you might be challenged to create an interior place of safety and comfort where gratefulness takes root and moments of deep quiet emerge. Yet, the benefits of doing so remain rich and satisfying.

When the mind quiets down a bit, you notice you can hear your heart's yearnings, griefs, and hurts. You can build a meaningful connection to your gut instincts or intuition. You could find yourself more easily inspired to the next love-filled action. Faith in something bigger than your fears begins to take hold. Your core can begin to feel strong, resilient, and free.

If you could draw a picture of this inner world, would it be filled with flowers, fields for dancing, open doors and windows for fresh breezes of ideas, a red Hippity Hop for laughter-filled bouncing, or new pebble pathways created by reverence and wonder? Could there be sculpted stone ceramics lining the grassy places where old hurts, fears, and resentments lay permanently at rest beneath the ground? Would all the boxes of lost treasure dreams finally be unpacked, ready to be heart gifts for beloved others? Can the energy debris from that critical voice be smudged out of the air and replaced with soap bubbles blown with compassion?

Accessing and intentionally creating the design of your internal hard drive can be some of the most healing, transformative, and liberating work of your life.

May you design your inner world in ways that enrich your faith, your love of life. May you live connected and centered in your beautiful interior world as you create a life you love living.
May you transform your life from the inside out.

Surfing the Net of Opportunity

"If you are serious about changing your life, you will find a way. If not, you will find an excuse."
—Jen Sincero

Ah, the obstacles and the opportunities! My latest challenge makes me laugh really hard. I declared this year to be one of growth for *Cherish Your World*, to be my highest and best in love and service to people. My word of the year is freedom. Freedom from the past, freedom to be, to breathe, to grow.

After weeks of intermittent Internet service that seemed to happen often when my laptop was in the mix, we discovered today that the problem might be because of me. I might have hit a key accidentally or attached too many documents to an email. I have had this conditioned reaction to immediately assume that when something doesn't work or goes 'wrong' that it's my fault. I think I'm the source, the cause. Untangling this reaction continues to take self-observation and self-compassion. I've learned that I make mistakes, but often I'm not the source of all the stressful happenings in life. I'm not that powerful. I also practice looking at challenges from different perspectives. I have become more curious rather than highly anxious.

I regularly look at them through the lens of feng shui wisdom. Belongings usually come with stories, memories, and associations. My laptop is no exception.

I received the MacBook Air as a Christmas gift instead of the anniversary ring I had asked for from my ex-husband. I'm forever grateful because I've chartered a new single life while relaunching *Cherish Your World* with this computer. I've written tips, blogs, articles, emails, and comments. I learned how to post photos I've taken. I've connected with many people on LinkedIn and Facebook using this important and powerful tool. After years of being terrified of technology, I've become a more confident, trusting, and willing student. I'm grateful for wonderful gurus in my network.

An anniversary ring would not have created these opportunities. When the marriage ended, I sold my wedding band to a jeweler at a fraction of its original value. An additional ring sale would not have funded the purchase of a computer. Those monies might only have purchased a couple delicious meals at a nice restaurant or a year's supply of chocolate.

I now faced a choice: hire Ghost Busters or gifted Reiki Healers for the current machine or purchase a new computer. My gut cheers loudly for a new laptop and a clean break with the past.

I might someday be gifted a ring and throw a Living in Love & Gratitude Party. In the meantime, I will navigate this latest curveball with humor, grace, and dignity. I'm thankful for those who created these machines that we count on to serve us. I believe I've earned a higher degree in letting go, though a committee likely still debates my status behind closed doors. I am ready to expand into a new brave world of this moment and the future.

Inner shifts lay the foundation for the outer shifts. In feng shui, technology breakdowns signal transformations. Electronics represent the fire element, in nature-sunshine, in humans- warmth, welcome, emotions, enthusiasm, and passion. Perfection. I am a woman on fire with growing emotional intelligence ready to be supported by a laptop that can meet me at this next leap of faith, of growth, and flight. I will meet you at the rocket ship launch!

May you keep stepping into the gap, navigating the obstacles between the life you used to live and your deepest, heartfelt desires and aspirations. May you keep going because your passion and clarity fuel your rocket ship.

Standing for Love

"Unexpected kindness is the most powerful, least costly, and most underrated agent of human change."
—Bob Kerrey

Standing at the intersection offers many insights that I continue to integrate into my heart as I hold a love sign with beloved friends in my community in North Carolina.

Visitors and neighbors walking through the intersection have taken our picture with their phones. Some have asked us what organization or church we are with and we reply, "none." One man got tears in his eyes when my friend replied, "We are standing for love, as simple as that." He asked her if he could hug her. She gave him a hug.

Two young teenage boys hopped off their bikes and declared, "Yes, I want a free hug!" We hugged them and then they quickly broke free and jumped back on their bikes to pedal away.

When asked curious questions of "why," we consistently reply, "We're standing for love."

A couple of weeks ago, a husband and wife surrounded by their children approached us with fierce opinions and angry questions. The wife kept undulating her body back and forth as she fired her repeated question at me. I noticed saliva gathered in the corner of her mouth as she sharply declared, "There is no love in the world!" I quietly listened. She fiercely spoke about people stealing homes, stealing belongings, and several religious themes. I agreed with her that love isn't stealing, that love isn't about violating healthy boundaries, that Jesus Christ definitely poured forth words of unconditional love when others spat on him and nails pierced his hands. Her body finally ceased to invade my private space; she appeared a tiny bit calmer.

"Did you feel heard?" I asked.

She turned and began walking away with her children. Barely turning around, she declared, "Yes. I felt heard."

Maybe you aren't inspired to stand with a "love" sign on a street corner or give free hugs, but know that your presence, your simple, kind acts of love and compassion matter in our world. For every act of unkindness, hatred, or violence, I know in my soul that there are millions of compassionate and caring moments being exchanged among people on this globe. The quiet helpers, first responders, ordinary yet extraordinary people show up offering their assistance and love where there's challenge, pain, and tragedy. Taking time to offer yourself as a humble servant of goodness in the ways that align with your heart and values matters. Small acts of kindness create a ripple of positivity in our world.

People have a flexible ribcage rather than a thick skull to protect their life-giving heart. There's movement in this most important muscle pulsing and sending oxygen-imbued blood to the cells along with an energy vibration out into the world. Filling your heart with gratitude and flowing out your kindness creates shifts like sunshine streaming through the clouds. Freeing yourself to give freely, generously can happen at any intersection where people meet hurt to heart.

May you be courageous for love during your dash between that birth date and death date. May you let people know how much you care through your unexpected compassion and kindness.

Becoming Whole

*"The curious paradox is that when I accept myself
just as I am, then I can change."*
—Carl Rogers

I recently was told that the reason I needed to hang a blanket over a large mirror facing my bed in a hotel room was because I wasn't willing to see things about myself, that I was avoiding parts of myself. Even when I shared that large mirrors in bedrooms kept me awake and disoriented, this person insisted that she could be in a war zone and be at peace. I noted internally that I had not asked for this feedback, yet she felt compelled to share it. I also observed how she later interacted with her ex-husband in a phone call and wondered about her claims of holding a peaceful countenance, no matter where she was.

This blanket scenario reminded me that we are all walking paradoxes. We say one thing that we believe is true about ourselves and then behave in exactly the opposite way, maybe even just moments later. Over the years, I've noticed a softening and releasing of my harsh judgments towards myself and others. I recognize an opening to an unfolding, an awakening to wholeness, a realization that I am clearly human and still capable of extraordinary acts of love and creative expression. And life experiences keep me humble quite regularly.

Years ago, I was in a discussion with two friends about tattoos and piercings. I listened as they shared their discomfort with individuals who wear body art, along with their awareness of the judgments they held about those who chose to be tattooed and pierced. I immediately realized that I may notice the outward appearance of a person, but I quickly shift to sensing their energy. My childhood training taught me to notice subtler cues about people.

I begin tracking individuals' behavior, how they treat other people in different settings, and how they treat themselves. I find myself observing their tone of voice, gestures, postures, body language, facial expressions, and the look in their eyes because this often reveals a great deal of information about people and about me as I continue to cultivate my "inner fly on the wall" that watches me be and do Laura. The paradox often reveals itself in people's tone of voice and the words they are saying, their ability to quickly alter into another persona, the words they speak and the very different choices they make.

I've met impeccably dressed people who are chronically angry and others who smell bad, dress poorly, and are the salt of the earth – kind and funny. I learned from my childhood experiences that people are not always who they appear to be in their clothes, words, and ways of showing up in the world.

Inconsistent behavior can show up in a moment, like the girls in high school who could be so kind to me one-on-one in the bathroom, but walk into the hallway, meet their friends, and suddenly spit out mean comments about my hair, blouse, or out-of-date knee socks.

Alternatively, there were those who could be syrupy kind in public and heinously cruel in private when no one else bore witness except me. And my son, as a schoolboy, observed that certain adults could be incredibly kind to other adults and be really cruel to children. He and I had numerous conversations about this dynamic, which happened to match many of my own experiences of adults when I was a child.

I learned quickly to look beyond how people dressed, how many tattoos they had, or how many cars they bragged about owning. What became important to me was to discover, to hold curiosity for the people they revealed themselves to be in all different types of situations. More important, I realized that I wanted to align myself with those valuable character qualities so I could be fully myself no matter where I was or with whom I interacted. I wanted to be the healthiest version of myself from the inside out.

Integrity, wholeness, owning the paradoxes in myself by seeing them with less shame and more lightheartedness continues to be the path that excites me. Evolving to embrace my humanity – the badass, dumbass, smartass, tenderass, cuteass, annoyedass, creativeass, comicalass, scaredass, "do I even have an ass?" from the inside frees me to choose to fuel the very essence of who I am as a Soul Self, a Higher Self who lives with dignity, humility and grace.

I probably won't get a tattoo, yet both my adult children have beautiful artwork permanently inked on their bodies. They also show up in the world as decent human beings with a great deal of love and compassion for others. After a brief rumination, I'll likely still cover a mirror in a hotel bedroom. At the same time, I will continue to be curious about my own reflection through compassionate eyes. I may sometimes wonder how others experience me and how each of us reveals who we are standing exposed in front of a mirror – willing to look at and embrace our vulnerable and brave, perfectly imperfect, beautiful selves.

Becoming Whole

May you catch yourself in the paradoxes and transcend these. May you know you are much more than pieces or parts. May you see yourself in your wholeness from the witness who watches you do and be you.

The World as You Are

"You do not see the world as it is.
You experience the world as you are."
—Unknown

Driving from North Carolina to Columbus, Ohio, on a crisp autumn day, I needed to make a quick biology stop. I pulled into a Pilot station and jogged to the women's restroom. I waited for the next available stall. The stall door opened. A sobbing woman walked out. Her false eyelash on her right eye had come detached. Tears streamed down her face.

"Are you okay?"

"My son died last night. You're not supposed to bury your children. He was 30 years old, a basketball player who stood six foot nine inches. I'm on the way to the morgue in Atlanta. He's been talking to me. His son, my grandson, found him. He died in his sleep. I don't want to go to the cemetery. My sister died last August. Oh, I can't do this. My boy. My boy. Oh, God...."

The words tumbled out of her at the pace of her tears streaming.

"Can I give you a hug?"

She opened her arms. We hugged, held each other as she continued to pour out her grief in sobs, words.

Softly I shared, "I almost lost my son twice. I can only imagine what you are actually living through. Oh, God, I'm so sorry. I'm here with you. You get to grieve. You love him so much. You will always love him. Love never ever dies. He loves you so much. He won't ever stop loving you. I know this."

"Thank you. I'm glad your son is alive. I don't even know who you are. You are being so kind. Oh, my son. You must go pee. I'm a nurse. Go pee."

In the stall, I continued to speak to her.

"You are so brave. You are a brave Momma. I know you can do this. You must grieve. You are so brave. You are here, alive."

I finished, washed my hands, and hugged and held her several more times while she poured out more words about her son, her sister, her job as a nurse, her nurse friend who was driving her to Atlanta.

I barely noticed the other women who quickly entered the stalls and disappeared. I pushed the heavy door open for her as we exited the restroom.

I immediately saw a young man mopping the floors right outside the restroom area. He saw the grieving woman and asked her, "Are you okay, Ma'am?"

I knew she hadn't heard him. I gently looked at his concerned eyes.

"Her son died last night."

"Oh, I am so sorry, Ma'am!"

She didn't hear his words, but I did. His empathy wrapped around his spoken words, an energy balm like a sun-warmed sandbag in the midst of her grief flood.

I held her hand as we walked by the aisles of colorfully packaged snacks. I opened the glass entrance door. She continued to cry and talk. We hugged one last time outside in the bright sunshine. I wished her courage, safe travels. I promised I would pray for her, her son, and her family.

Back in my car, tears welled up in my eyes as I shared briefly with my Sweet Love what had just transpired.

I realized I had held space, that I hadn't internalized her grief, which is what I would have done in the past as the unhealthy empath I used to be. I noticed that my practices of flowing through my own grief waves allowed me to embrace a complete stranger with much compassion.

Inside each of these interactions including the young man who shared his heartfelt condolences with a stranger, God gave me beautiful signs that I actually matter, that I belong to the human family. I've struggled with doubts about my right to exist, my sense of value, for too long. Centering in faith and love, I asked to be humble enough to finally put to rest the experience of unworthiness, all the accompanying body postures associated with this, and birth an enduring, unshakeable inner experience of being enough.

The tenderness and grace gifted to me by a nurse in the ER who hugged and held me when I wept with a grief-terror for my own son flowed freely forward to this beautiful, grieving nurse, a mother, a member of my ever-expanding human family. Her raw, vulnerable, grieving heart connected with mine in the very core of our shared humanity. I live utterly grateful for these blessings.

Paying attention beyond our own needs requires an expanded view of the world, a commitment to focus out on what's happening around us. The opportunities to make a positive difference remain countless when we experience an expanded way of living, the you and me of the we, sourced from the essential self and a place of openheartedness and robust inner equanimity.

The World as You Are

May you naturally pour forward the compassion you've received as a natural expression of your goodness and wholeheartedness. May you know you touch the lives of many with your loving energy presence.

From Traumas to Quiet Triumph

"Going to the mountains is going home."
—John Muir

I met with friends in Columbus for dinner to celebrate my upcoming relocation to the mountains of North Carolina. I had only lived in central Ohio.

As we ate our vegan dishes, one friend asked me, "What are you looking forward to the most?"

I sat silently for a moment. "I'm looking forward to uncoiling."

A great deal that had happened in my recent past, in my long-ago past, imbued my life with a chronic backdrop of not ever feeling safe. Having endured many traumas and seemingly endless violations of my boundaries, I really didn't know what it could be like to live in a place devoid of triggers: people, places, experiences, reminders, and memories.

Thankfully, I dedicated half of my life to many various forms of healing modalities, which will continue to support me for a lifetime. My inner world has been coming alive for years as a safe haven, an expanded place of sacred discoveries, clutter clearings, and reconnections to pieces of goodness that I had kept stored away. Like a ball of twine, my nervous system continues to be blessed to uncoil in the quiet beauty of the mountains.

I feel like I'm finally reveling in what I've heard others discover when they move away and geographically break free from their past, their history, and all the existing painful reminders everywhere. Over the last several months, I have unpacked countless experiences that I had shelved or simply didn't have time or space to examine.

When my former mother-in-law passed away two months ago, I finally fully grieved the loss of that entire family. Though their choice to cut ties with me felt like yet another rejection and abandonment, I love them all to this day. I may never understand in my mind the choice they made, but my heart simply had to grieve, to flow through the actual hurt their rejection represented. I had to learn to be brave in the wilderness of isolation from them. I keep bringing myself back to recognizing that home exists in my soul.

I finally cut the noose of unworthiness and toxic shame that had suffocated me for years. I found a richer voice of truth and a renewed ability to breathe from my diaphragm. A deeper dive into my long-ago difficult past to reclaim the treasures of my lost childhood continues to be rewarding and liberating. A couple of days ago, I could actually feel and "see" all my inner children joyfully rushing towards my grownup self for a great big bear hug. Now they feel more convinced of their safety and belonging. I get to let them know we're turning all that hard stuff they endured into prose, poetry, and hilarious comedy that makes people laugh.

Hearing the birds singing as I sit in front of three walls of windows that face trees, leaves, blossoms, and rolling mountains, I feel a profound sense of contentment. Deep inside I have an unshakeable knowing that my life will not ever return to what it was. Receiving the abundant love that fills my life at present allows me to continue to give of myself generously in love and service. I am becoming in my life what I choose to experience in our world. This choice lives as a quiet triumph and an answer to the whispering, pleading mantras of all my inner children. I am at peace.

May you find comfort and safety in your own skin and in your life circumstances. May this create the foundation for deeper healing and transformations.

Breakthroughs in Being Alive

"When we deny our stories, they define us. When we run from struggle, we are never free.
So, we turn toward the truth and look it in the eye. We will not be characters in our stories.
Not villains, not victims, not even heroes. We are the authors of our lives. We write our own daring endings."
—*Brené Brown*

I learned about Landmark Education from my former brother-in-law. He handed me a brochure as my second husband, and I drove away to celebrate our honeymoon in Bar Harbor, Maine, and Acadia National Park. I thanked him, then shoved the red-and-white pamphlet into the glove compartment. Out of sight. Out of mind. A year later, I pulled it out while waiting for some friends. I read the entire pamphlet knowing I wanted to participate. This was the first time I heard about transformation. I registered for the Landmark Forum, walked into the room, and began to engage with all the ways I pretend in life. I began to discover what I didn't know that I didn't know about myself, about being human, and endless possibilities. I completed the curriculum for living, numerous seminars, the Communications course, the Wisdom course, and Power and Contribution.

After a decade of intellectual distinguishing, declaring possible ways of being, completing lots of homework, which included looking straight into the eyes of my past experiences through the power of language reframes, I noticed that terror and rage still lived in my body.

I began engaging somatic work including cranio-sacral therapy (CST) and somatic trauma resolution (STR) with two gifted practitioners. I read many books including *I Hate You, Don't Leave Me* by Jerold Jay Kreisman, *Understanding the Borderline Mother* by Christine Lawson, and *Surviving the Borderline Parent* by Roth and Friedman. These books, especially the latter two, validated many of my experiences as a child, the heinous dynamics of my childhood environment, and the painful chaos that had created many moments of terror inside me that I lived with every single night and day for as long as I can remember ... until I didn't.

During this time period, I accessed internal tracking tools and practices to clip lines leading to the explosive bombs of the "fight" reaction. I thawed the numbing dissociation of the "freeze" reaction. I began the courageous, rigorous work of healing the persistent traumatic stress. Within a couple of years, I ended contact with all members of my family of origin, knowing I had to break the cycle to create healthy, vibrant relationships with my two growing children as best as I could. I had hoped to do the same with their dad, but this aspiration did not transpire.

In the therapists' offices I cussed, shook, and sometimes puked. I wept and screamed. At home, I put myself in "time out" when I felt the triggers fire in my body. I sobbed and screamed into pillows. I did everything I could to keep my son and daughter safe from my inner demons. I took full responsibility for my past words and deeds. I took detox baths while weeping into the hot, steamy water. I began to forgive myself, to love myself, to see that I mattered. Deep inner work of this magnitude is not for cowards, going through all the muck is the only way.

Identifying all traumatic events of my past, which included many that happened outside my childhood household, allowed me to see the experiences fully, to no longer deny that they had happened, and to finally flow through the grief that accompanied all those shocks to the nervous system. The involved process of triage for my amygdala while rewiring my nervous system began to free me. Pathways opened to the prefrontal cortex as my life shifted into sustained periods of calm. Meditating, being grateful, dancing, doing yoga, exercising, and living with embodied awareness became daily or weekly experiences that deepened my healing. Multiple pathways created this inner transformation of living more moments of most days with profound and enduring equanimity.

I know for certain that my life is a testament to transformation. I have broken through the experience of living as a traumatized, terrorized, people-pleasing victim pretending to be someone who had it all together. I no longer live in constant fear. I sleep free of night terrors. I am unrecognizable to my former selves.

Do you wake up in the morning in love with your life? Do you experience quiet in your mind with an unshakeable sense of purpose in your feet? Do you feel deep peace inside your body as you move through the experiences of your day? Do you even know that this feeling is possible? What if your experience of being alive could be peaceful? Would that be an unrecognizable shift in your reality?

You may or may not have endured traumas, but you may live with substantial anxiety. Thriving from the inside out is possible. You don't have to die to rest in peace. You'll likely have to process through bottled-up emotional content. Burning through this pain in your heart can liberate you. The willingness and passion to transform resides in every one of us.

Nothing may change in your outside world. There will be bills to pay, toilets to clean, food to purchase, dishes to wash, and work to do, but your experience of flowing through these tasks could alter to one of appreciation and love. This experience is possible.

May you find your pathway to healing, to transforming from the inside out because the quality of your life is worth it. May you know you are important to many lives that you touch every single day. May you recognize that your being healthy creates a whole new glorious vibration of joy in our world.

Live an Ordinary, Exceptional Life

*"Before death takes away what you are given,
give away what there is to give."*
—*Rumi*

My dad died a few days before Labor Day after 89 years of life. I celebrate my dad by sharing with you some of the lessons I learned from the way he lived, the man I experienced, the actions he took, the gentle presence he had, the courageous ideas he shared with others, and the pathways of possibility he opened. I know that much of who I am today is because of my dad.

If fathers are here to teach us how to leave a legacy, ways to be in the larger world, then my dad modeled this passionately. He served as a math professor at Ohio Wesleyan University. He coached the summer swim team. As the chairman of the local Democratic Party for over two decades in our community, he bravely took the heat from many who disagreed with his principles, his belief in the worth and dignity of every person, and his stand for equality, social justice, democracy, civil discourse, and freedom. He mastered the art of agreeing to disagree. He honored the dignity of other people as he cultivated the ability to focus on ideas separate from the person who spoke them.

When he lost the chairmanship to another man, he stood up, walked over, shook his hand, and said, "I make this election unanimous."

I witnessed this generous concession when I served as an elected precinct representative. With that gracious action, he modeled integrity and strength of character. He became someone others respected even if they disagreed with his ideas. Because he saw people as individuals who deserved to be seen, heard, and valued, my dad gained the esteem of many different people of all walks of life in our community. He really listened to people. I witnessed these qualities in his teaching, activism, and coaching. As best as he could, he listened to me as his daughter. Emerging from his own struggles, he learned to be a decent person.

He'd been bullied as a boy for his small stature. He stood a lean 5'6" as an adult. As a boy, he was often the smallest in his classroom. He learned to use his words, to walk away, to run. His favorite childhood book was *The Story of Ferdinand* by Munro Leaf, a story of a bull who preferred to smell the flowers and to sit peacefully in a field, rather than fight in bullfights. Dad struggled with his ability to read. With support, he overcame these challenges. In college at Oberlin, he excelled as a student athlete. He earned a Ph.D. in mathematics from The Ohio State University.

In his 50s, my dad began participating in triathlons, marathons, and biathlons. He won his age group competition at many of these events. In his 60s, he competed in the Hawaii Iron Man twice. The first time, he collapsed a mile from the finish line. "I stopped having fun" is what my dad said. My mom shared that he'd been taken to the medical tent for dehydration, lack of nutrition. When he returned the second time, he crossed that finish line at 64 years old. For those of you who may not know, this race consists of swimming in the ocean for 2.4 miles, followed by cycling for 112 miles, and ending with a marathon run of 26.2 miles. There's no napping between each part.

His passion for athletics flowed into his work for the community Parks and Recreation Department as he joined others in creating a sprint triathlon for adults and children. Designed to welcome first-time participants, families, and seasoned athletes, this event became a yearly experience open to all. At first called the Tree Triathlon, this event was renamed The Dave Staley triathlon, in honor of my dad. I was fortunate to compete in the Dave Staley triathlon three years in a row, to be there when the 35th annual event took place.

What will endure in my heart are my dad's courage, gentleness, deep inner strength, and dignity – how he wept openly, laughed loudly, listened deeply, especially when others fiercely disagreed with him; when he often stood alone for what he valued, for what he knew was the right thing to do.

May my life, the brave, unconventional choices I have made, the way I conduct myself with others be a part of his legacy. Dad, I know that you have given much to our world in how you lived your life. Thank you for living such an ordinary, exceptional life, for inviting others to do the same in their way, in their time. I love you.

May you participate fully in life. May you laugh from your belly at yourself. May you listen deeply to other points of view with respect. May you live true to your heart's passions.

Get Your House in Order

"Learn to live as though you are facing death at all times, and you'll become bolder and more open. If you live life fully, you won't have any last wishes. You will have lived them every moment."
—*Michael Singer from The Untethered Soul*

I received a phone call that the owner of the house I am currently renting in North Carolina is selling the property. I may have to move from this beautiful house because the new owner may not lease the home. This uncertainty opens my heart to savoring all the moments in this space, to appreciate the funky black & white paisley wallpaper in the half bathroom, the dark baby-poop brown on the walls of the dining and living room, and the many windows that face the living artwork of trees, sky, mountains, birds, squirrels, rabbits, butterflies, hummingbirds, and black bears.

One morning I learned about a property for rent. I drove up to a home that had a Shel Silverstein poem,

The Tree House, on a placard next to the front door. This immediately felt like a wonderful sign, a good omen. I parked my Subaru under a carport, which would keep vehicles dry during rain and thunderstorms. Entering this house, I immediately noticed the nook with a bench and hooks, which I loved. This reminded me of when my kids were little, that transition place for taking off shoes or boots, removing coats, and having a place to rest for a moment. This tree house has many windows with beautiful views of the mountains and trees. Many rooms, lots of space, two levels create an inviting, even enchanting home. I still love the house of joy on the side of a mountain where a momma deer and her two babies visited on Christmas Eve day.

There are friends convinced the Universe wants me to live in an even better space. I don't know. Mostly, I've concluded that home remains inside the very core of my being, that awakened place that watches this lively movie of my life, and that anticipates with curiosity the next adventure. Living amongst the mountains continues to nourish my soul. Every single day of my life now feels more precious than the one before. All the cells of my body, mind, heart, and spirit understand that life is now. I will leave this planet in the middle of the movie even though I want to see it to the very happy, beloved ones laughing, dancing, hugging, celebrating, singing in a field of sunflowers next to the mountains, glorious ending.

Get Your House in Order

For some people, hearing "get your house in order" scares them as they think their death is imminent. And maybe it is. Others don't clear their clutter because they have the belief that if they clear, they will die. Well, here's what I know. We are all going to die. And you might die right after clearing your clutter or you might not. Is your space in harmony with your heart? Are you living in alignment from the inside out? Have you created a life that you love living and will enjoy for however many days you do have left? Is dying your greatest fear? Or is living full out with love bursting from your heart, gratitude exuding from your being, and joy dancing in your toes your greatest fear?

I know that there are plenty of people who live vibrantly alive with very little clutter. Maybe you are one. Some of those folks can be a bit uptight as they may not have gotten their hearts or souls cleaner and clearer of past hurts, pains, insecurities, and harsh criticisms. They don't want you touching anything in their space. They've roped off the pristine living room. Others who live with little or no clutter have found great alignment in living clearer outside and inside of themselves. They may live to 105 years old or die in three days. We don't know.

I also have observed that some people who live with a lot of clutter have gotten stuck. For those who feel a bit stagnant in their lives, the clutter may have a suffocating impact. They may wonder why they feel "meh," lifeless, numb, or already dead. People living in clear spaces may also have this challenge because the experience of life comes from the inside of you. The transformation can happen when you recognize death as your favorite teacher, that the most important shift takes place from your inner wakeful noticing of the miracle of being alive. And the belongings likely will outlive you.

What if you really did have only a week to live? Would you shift your actions? Would you finally speak what your heart has wanted to say all your life? Would you stop complaining about the rain and feel excited to get soaking wet because it meant you were healthy enough to walk outside? Would you host a gratitude, giveaway party for all those unused belongings that could be enjoyed by your neighbors, friends, and family who will go on living?

Can you even imagine not being able to taste that first sip of coffee or tea or orange juice? Can you imagine not being able to look into the eyes of your beloved ones, to hug them, to tell them with your own voice, "*I love you with all my heart!!*"? Can you imagine not ever holding hands with the deliciousness of this life? What are you doing to savor each and every moment of your sacred, beautiful life?

For me "get your house in order" is a wakeup invitation to appreciate from the very core of your being as many moments of your life as you can, to celebrate that you have an abundance of belongings (for those of you who have this!). Expressing a rich life often involves taking new actions in this moment to live like it matters, thankful that you can breathe, that you can unburden your heart of all that never wanted to permanently reside there.

May you live inspired to clear your space to reflect the harmony you are feeling in your heart. May you continue a joyful expansion of your inner and outer worlds because you want to live free, unburdened, awake, alive for as many days as you are fortunate to be on this planet swirling through the galaxies.

Weaving Themes Together

"You were born with potential. You were born with goodness and trust. You were born with ideals and dreams. You were born with greatness. You were born with wings. You are not meant for crawling, so don't. You have wings. Learn to use them and fly."
—Rumi

A couple years ago, I began the first of three emotional intelligence and leadership courses with Next Level Trainings in Columbus, Ohio. In each of these experiences – Discovery, Breakthrough, and the Vision Impact Program – I grabbed the opportunity to see and release limiting beliefs; to process through crusty, unresolved emotional residue; to take courageous, unfamiliar actions for my life, my vision for our world; and as a team member to raise money for Big Brothers, Big Sisters of Central Ohio to support children of incarcerated parents, so these children could attend summer camp along with being matched with a Big Brother or Sister.

With the wise and gentle guidance of coaches and trainers, I found my way home to my soul. Tearfully united with a being I hadn't completely seen through eyes of value and love until that sacred moment, I broke free to breathe and be. Gratitude will not ever be a big enough word for what I feel every single day I live. I now know in my cells that every moment contains gifts, lessons, richness. The opportunity to live a transformed life imbued with faith, love, and courage became a channel I could no longer block or resist.

Dismantling limiting mental constructs, the seemingly endless network of untrue thoughts that spin a web-like world inside your mind, can begin a journey towards a quiet space of your own inner witness.

Carrying boxes and bags of unwanted, unloved belongings that clog the rooms of your home, office, and garage complements the labor of love to the inner quiet place, to live with breathing room and clarity.

Clearing your calendar of obligations that create cranky resentment expands a holistic experience of healing and transformation of space, mind, body, heart, and soul. As you continue asking yourself why you are here on the planet and what's the joy-filled, heart-led purpose of your life, you can listen with curious, rapt attention.

Bravely walking towards life-giving, meaningful, laughter-filled quality relationships with people, you attract who you are at your essence. You observe that being celebrated feels much better than being denigrated or being mean to yourself. You begin to see yourself in everyone you meet.

You can begin to practice living from inspiration as you take a deep breath and look for what's possible or from the grief-love present in exhaled sobs of suffering. The cornucopia of your inner being, thought-filled mind, topsy-turvy or pristine home, places you visit or live, people you encounter, and the events of your life invite you to a meaningful conversation with your heart. Looking from any or all of these domains, you can begin to release the limiting beliefs about yourself that were never true and finally feel the full range of emotions as they flow through you. Consciously choosing a love-filled life, an inspired life, involves an inner shift. You most likely will notice a gap. I hope you can mind the gap between your outside world and your inner sanctuary. Cultivating the inner qualities of courage, gratitude, resilience, honesty, self-love, self-compassion, and self-worth can support you closing that gap while opening you to love-filled experiences of being alive.

As I drill down to the core of all the themes and messages in this book, I realize I want you to know in your bones that you are not alone, that you matter to our world, that you can heal your hurts and heartbreak, that transformation from the inside out is possible, that you can clear all forms of clutter, and that your heart has amazing things to tell you about who you are and why you are here. Your heart won't ever lead you astray. You are bigger than anything that ever happened to you.

You are loved more than you can even imagine. If no one ever said that to you, I'm saying these words to you, to your heart right now. Love always finds a way to love. I love you. I celebrate your courage in living true, in living awake, in living joyously, and in living beyond what you thought was possible for your life.

May the words that have opened your heart support your brave journey. May your insights, feelings, and deeper truths become a guide leading you home. May your answers to the questions create a roadmap to your unique, beautiful, and inspired life.

Breathe and Be

Let love open you
Like a flower softly blooming
Rose red unfurling,
Releasing a sweet scent
Into our world.

Let love strengthen you
Like a fragile, brave butterfly
Cracking its
Cocoon.

Let love touch your skin,
Seep into your soul,
Purify your heart like
Sunshine streaming through
Raindrops creating rainbows
Bending with color in
A thunderhead filled sky.

Let love free you
To fly gracefully on
The winds of wisdom.

*Breathe and
Be in
Love.*

AFTERWORD

"The best and most beautiful things
in the world cannot be seen or even touched;
they must be felt with the heart."
—Helen Keller

Waking up to the sound of birds chirping with sunlight streaming in the windows, I notice I'm gently invited to a new day of being alive. My body naturally knows morning has arrived. I'm not certain when I mostly refrained from using an alarm clock. When I moved to the mountains, I brought a clock radio with large bright red numbers on the face. Preferring complete darkness, cold, and quiet, I eventually donated the clock radio. If I need an alarm, I use my phone, which remains outside the bedroom. I've discovered I prefer to hear live birds.

The alarm clock represents an influence, something made by humans that can impact behavior. The mechanical object replaces the influence of another human being, who presumably has an agenda and an expectation that you get your body out of bed. Sometimes the human "alarm clock" may not be reliable, trustworthy, compassionate, or kind. The mechanical object probably became a more reliable substitute for the human version, especially if you live alone. In either case, influence rather than inspiration entered the world of waking up.

I have been reflecting deeply for years about being inspired rather than being influenced. Influence remains a human invention designed by and for other humans. Usually influence involves agendas, expectations, power, and control accompanied by a great deal of attachment to outcomes, which may be positive, negative, or simply unintended. One definition for influence is "the capacity or power to be a compelling force on or produce effects on the actions, behaviors, opinions of others."

In this definition, there's no value infusion. Influence might look like talking heads doing mental gymnastics with vision, courage, vulnerability, fears, unresolved or unmet needs, insecurities, judgments, demands, and persistent internal "shoulds" and "should nots." Influence can come from fear, love, or a confusing mixture of the two with a consistent agenda within all these pathways. Thus, an influencer could be one who has a life-giving, a harmful, or a confusing agenda. Throughout our human history, we've experienced all types. Influence remains quite distinct from inspiration.

Inspiration lives in a much wider, broader, deeper, and expansive place than influence. Inspiration can come from inside human hearts. Inspiration feels grounded in emotion and often results in human creative expression, innovation, acts of compassion, beauty, and kindness. Some might say that inspiration comes from God, the Universe, or a quiet mind. Sometimes inspiration seems magical and otherworldly. Inspiration can come from anywhere and can involve everything.

Sources of inspiration can include blooming brilliant red roses or a breathtaking sunset over the ocean. The feel of a pet curling up in your lap, a tender, loving kiss, the sound of babies laughing, music that makes your body want to dance and make love, the sight of a gorgeous painting of the mountains at dusk, a poem, a smile on the face of a beloved one can all ignite inspiration. Engaging the senses of sight, smell, taste, touch, sound, or inner awareness of body sensations including gut instincts, goosebumps, or heart whisperings, an experience of your whole body in relationship to everything around you can allow you to access this expanded world. "A sudden, brilliant, creative, or timely idea" and "the excitement of the mind or emotions to a high level of feeling or activity" are two definitions that leaped off the thin paper page of a dictionary. All inspire.

Being inspired rarely involves fear, anger, revenge, depression, loneliness, grief, or some hidden agenda.

Inspiration may be informed by these darker places and often appears for human beings as we yearn to be whole and at peace. Being inspired in heart, mind, and body often results in a desire to express and create from the truth of pain, the giddiness of joy, and a burning desire to be free. There's an emancipation of the soul, a life being awakened from the inside to the outside and untethered. Inspiration can feel playful, joyful, awake – a tender underbelly of what really enlivens your being. Inspiration allows the "soft animal of your body to love what it loves." (Mary Oliver)

The sun shines without ever saying to the earth, trees, plants, wildlife and humans, "You owe me." A swan will not ever lecture you about how to sit up straight, laugh like a "lady," or refrain from talking with your mouth full of food. Roses won't ever use flattery to cause you to be courageous or charm you to trust them or convince you to just "be genuine." Your dog or cat is unlikely to hold a meeting about how you can improve your listening or speaking skills. The wild geese goslings won't demand that you behave just like they do or expect you to water the grass they eat. You might live in awe of these adorable babies and be moved to care for this shared world of food, water, and light.

May you inhale deeply as you receive the breath of life from all the places that source creative ideas. May these ideas consistently uplift your life and the lives of others, spark the inner truth of knowing how beautiful and brave you really are, how you can transform yourself to live free in love, light, wonder, awe, and grace. May you live inspired.

ACKNOWLEDGMENTS

A Grateful Heart

To the many different people from all walks of life with whom I've been fortunate to cross paths: Thank you for the rich lessons you brought to my life about being human, healing, living true, and loving myself and other people.

To Martha Beck, Gabrielle Bernstein, Brené Brown, Deepak Chopra, Alan Cohen, Terah Kathryn Collins, the late Pat Conroy, Serena Dyer Posini, the late Dr. Wayne Dyer, Elizabeth Gilbert, the late Louise Hay, Esther Hicks, Karen Kingston, Denise Linn, Tosha Silver, Jen Sincero, Michael Singer, Cheryl Strayed, Oprah Winfrey: All your words continue to inspire my evolution as a spiritual being having a human experience, my burning passion to share my voice with the world. Because of all of you, I freely, fearlessly, and passionately share my truth and wisdom.

To all my social media connections, followers, and friends: Thank you for being your unique selves, for inspiring me with your posts and photos; for all the "likes," "loves," and kind, meaningful comments; for receiving my likes, loves, and reflections.

To all my clients and workshop participants: You open your homes and lives to me and remain receptive to my guidance and aware of the wisdom inside your hearts. I'm grateful for your honest sharing of your challenges, dreams, heartaches, and heartwarming stories of home and life transformations. Thank you for running with the ideas we discuss to create spaces that inspire lives you love living from the inside out. Your actions inspire me deeply. To work with you continues to be a privilege and an honor.

To Dr. Alison Hazelbaker, Kristen Peairs, Grace Scarbrough, Pamela Shook, and Mary Ware: Your multifaceted gifts continue to support my life transformations. Your ability to facilitate, hold space, guide, and bear witness allow me to flourish in this bonus round of being alive. Thank you from my body, mind, heart, and soul.

To Rev. Patricia Cagganello, CEO and Founder of Sacred Stories Publishing, and your amazing staff: Thank you for your belief in my writing, and your wisdom, support, and kindness in navigating the publishing world as beautiful, collaborative partners on this adventure.

To Susan Rooks, the Grammar Goddess: Thank you for your expert editing skills, keen insights, honest feedback, and friendship.

To Dennis Pitocco, Founder, BizCatalyst360: Thank you for being a champion of my writing as well as the wonderful writing of many individuals whose important, cutting-edge, and inspiring ideas can be made available to a global audience. I deeply appreciate the opportunity to work with you, to be your friend. Thank you for introducing me to Rev. Patricia Cagganello.

To Rebecca Alben, Abe Alexander, Patrick Anderson, Angie Bailey, Dean Bailey, Shelley Brown, Eric Clark, Elba Colon, Alnoor Damji, Timothy DeHart, Christopher Hawker, Jacob Kolinko, Jim Kopasko, Kori Keck, Ken Lazar, Chris Lee, Helen Neumann, Debbie Stohl, Michael Strasner, Bob Up, VIP Soul Nova Loves, Tom Wentz, Jeff Young: You hold me high. You raise me up when I've fallen in the mud or have struggled to see my worth. Because of your enduring kindness, support, laughter, honesty, guidance, wisdom, and love, I now live on a side of a mountain with wings for soaring like a seagull or sometimes even a great blue heron.

To Bill Altork, Jim Carrilion, Mamie Davis Hilliard, Larry Pearlman, Damaris Pierce, Carolyn Shorkey, Ann Sillman: Thank you my beloved poets, for your warm welcome, loving presence, beautiful poetry, acceptance, and kind, honest feedback. In the gentle space of all of you, I allowed a poet's voice to grow strong and clear.

To Vanessa Bey, Cathy Davis, Teresa DeVitt, Don Fortner, Doug Grossman, Ann Joyce, Susie Kalyn, Rae Larson, Barb Marshall, Sandy Zimlich: Thank you all for being my beloved ones, accepting me exactly as I am, believing in me, listening with presence and non-judgment, for being your beautiful selves and gracing my life with your enduring love. Each of you is a precious gift in my life. Your love surrounds the words that pour out of me.

To Ruth Marian Pittard, Ruby: Thank you for your wisdom, the rich blessing of your love and friendship, your unwavering belief in me. Thank you for being a beautiful soul, for your passionate commitment to love in our community and the world.

To Julianna Hausman and Matthew Hausman: Thank you for receiving my perfectly imperfect ways of loving both of you from the moment you were born to this very day and beyond. The sacred gift of being your mom continues to enrich my life every single day as your souls came to teach me about patience, presence, non-judgment, joy, courage, and unwavering, unconditional love.

To Paul Hall: Thank you for being you, for communicating in all love languages, for holding me, accepting me, choosing me, and receiving my love. Because of our beautiful love relationship, I joyfully dance in peace, safety, grace. You had my heart at Mary Oliver.

ABOUT THE AUTHOR

The founder of Cherish Your World, Laura Staley passionately helps people thrive by guiding them to a holistic transformation of space, heart, mind, body, and soul. Laura knows that there's a relationship between the conditions of our homes or workplaces and the quality of our lives. Trained and certified with the Western School of Feng Shui and seasoned by almost two decades of working with a variety of clients, Laura uses her intuition and expertise to empower her clients to produce remarkable results in their lives. Her trifecta of serving people includes speaking, writing, and compassionate listening.

As a columnist, Laura writes personal essays focused on self-discovery, feng shui, emotional health, and transformations from the inside out. Laura is a published author of two books: Let Go Courageously and Live with Love: Transform Your Life with Feng Shui and the Cherish Your World Gift Book of 100 Tips to Enhance Your Home and Life.

Prior to creating her company, Laura worked as a full-time parent and an assistant professor at Ohio Wesleyan University. She earned a Ph.D. in political science from The Ohio State University. Her joys in life include laughing with loved ones, dancing, reading, meditating, running, being in nature, and listening to music she loves. She resides in Black Mountain, North Carolina with her lovable dog, Layla.

You are welcome to connect with Laura at CherishYourWorld.com and LoveYourSpaceLoveYourLife.com

www.ingramcontent.com/pod-product-compliance
Lightning Source LLC
Chambersburg PA
CBHW030147100526
44592CB00009B/164